BECOMING LUCIFERIAN MAGICK

The foundations and essential ideological beginnings of theory and initial practice of Luciferian Magick and Sorcery. This book is meant as a guide and theological assumption of the reasoning behind the practice of Magick from an Adversarial or Rebellious paradigm against spiritual union with a higher power.

BY

MICHAEL W. FORD

Edited by J. Poirot (Fra:Dualkarnain)

TITLES BY MICHAEL W. FORD

THE BIBLE OF THE ADVERSARY

LUCIFERIAN WITCHCRAFT

SATANIC MAGICK: A Paradigm of Therion

GATES OF DOZAK: Primal Sorcery

THE VAMPIRE GATE: The Vampyre Magickian

BOOK OF THE WITCH MOON

THE FIRST BOOK OF LUCIFERIAN TAROT

LUCIFERIAN TAROT

LUCIFERIAN GOETIA: A Book of Howling

ADAMU: Luciferian Sex Magick

LIBER HVHI: Magick of the Adversary

Please visit our website: www.luciferianwitchcraft.com

BEGINNING LUCIFERIAN MAGICK

MICHAEL W. FORD

Edited by J. Poirot (Fra:Dualkarnain)

Dedicated to those who seek
To enter the darkness,
To discover and bring forth light

BEGINNING LUCIFERIAN MAGICK
By Michael W. Ford
Edited by J. Poirot (Fra:Dualkarnain)

Copyright © 2008 by Michael W. Ford

All rights reserved. No part of this book, in part or in whole, may be reproduced, transmitted, or utilized, in any form or by any means electronic or mechanical, including photocopying, recording, or by any information storage and retrieval system, without written permission in writing from the publisher, except for brief quotations in critical articles, books and reviews.

Second edition 2008 Succubus Productions
ISBN 978-1-4357-1645-2

Information:

Succubus Productions
PO Box 926344
Houston, TX 77292
USA

Website: http://www.luciferianwitchcraft.com
email: succubusproductions@yahoo.com

BEGINNING LUCIFERIAN MAGICK

TABLE OF CONTENTS

1. INTRODUCTION 7
2. **INTERPRETING THE ADVERSARY** 8
3. MAGICKAL FOUNDATIONS 17
4. ADVERSARIAL PANTHEONS 23
5. CONCEPTS OF INITIATION 39
6. PRACTICING MAGICK CONSISTENTLY 55
7. ALTAR & TOOLS 56
8. RITUAL CONSTRUCTION 64

APPENDIX: LEGACY OF THE LEFT HAND PATH 105

INTRODUCTION

The Luciferian Path is one which exercises the sanctification of Self by activating aspects of the Adversary in particular form. This approach, highly at odds with traditional occult assumptions, is difficult to navigate for Practitioners just getting started.

Questions arise such as:
> What is Adversarial Magick?
>
> What distinguishes it from other paths?
>
> What can be expected by its practice?
>
> How does one decide if it is personally suitable?
>
> Who or what are the deities of the Adversarial pantheon and how does one approach them?
>
> What steps can be taken to start the journey?

These are the questions this manuscript answers. The first part of this book deals with theoretical and methodological foundations of magick. The second part takes a look at previous books through ritual, commentary and suggested practices. Reprinted works have been refocused and expounded upon with additional instructions for the beginner.

Previous works of the author were initially written to organize a record of personal magickal practice. Ancient magickal forms were revived and new ways of magickal approach were synthesized. These practices became further activated by the technical meritocracy of chaos magick fusing with philosophical and Gnostic elements of Satanism.

A progressive, system of initiatory magick was thus born. Heralding the spirit of Lucifer through Adversarial forms, it is now necessary to make this decidedly-complex path accessible to each man and woman with an interest in Self-Deification.

INTERPRETING THE ADVERSARY

The Luciferian Path offers a unique approach to life and darkness. Its doctrines are free of dogma and cults of personality. This fundamental cultural shift in dark-initiatory magick often creates interpretive challenges for the new Practitioners.

Understanding and beginning the path requires a significant investment of time and focus. Once accepted and possessed, the Initiate transforms into One of the Witchblood. All obstacles barring the way become illuminated into that which must be torn, clawed and rent on each individual's ascent to Godhood. May this work constitute an illuminating beacon making these first steps more clear.

The path of Yatuk Dinoih witchery demands the overcoming of opposites, not only to unite but to master and compel. The unseen death, as it has been referred to, is essentially the Adverse Current found in the methodology of the Hebraic Qlippoth. This fountain of the vampire is the consuming energy which builds the mind and spirit of the Black Adept. The Initiate gains *afterknowledge* (atavisms) and *foreknowledge* of Ahriman. The symbolism of the Four Hells is a model for willing and commanding change to occur. The Luciferian Path is vast, but you don't have to concern yourself with the breadth of it all just yet.

Starting off in Luciferian Magick is to strive for challenge that manifests into self-illumination. Starting upon the path, one must understand the difference between symbol and significance.

It is important to note that the ideas outlined here are but guidelines. Each Initiate must take these ideas and possess them- make them your own. Change each and every part to suit your person, prefence and ascent. Achieve the greatest magnitude and intensity as possible.

It is easy to let words and terminologies distract you from the deeper meanings in these doctrines. There is a natural tendency of the mind to focus on deciding whether you agree with the correctness of a particular word or concept. Such a "judgment-decision" focus can sabotage the ability to comprehend the depth of the ideas and relationships communicated.

Let us consider that a word is merely a symbol. A symbol has a unique set of attributes. The symbol has a peculiar relationship to other symbols. Pay particular attention to these relationships and the actions connecting each symbol. This way of looking at the Luciferian Doctrines can be of great assistance in grasping the practical framework of Adversarial Magick.

It is just like deciding to learn a new language. It takes study and practice. Fastidious mapping out and writing down new words, defining them with ones you already understand. One becomes an effective communicator when concepts can be shared across symantic and symbolic boundaries.

Boundaries, as languages, exist within (and beyond) Self to understand and breach. Once emphasis is redirected from "judgment-decision" into "essence-focus-action" can these boundaries be understood, confronted and transcended. This is done through the art of symbol, ritual, energy and action.

Each individual possesses a unique set of internal languages with their own attributes, restrictions and drives. Some are banal and animalistic while others are mental and even spiritual. As languages and attributes vary by person, they are impossible to index on a wide scale. **Such is the reason that systems of symbols are employed!**

Just like learning a new language, consider the common behaviors between geographically-dispersed cultures. Such behaviors include protecting one's family, provisional roles of males and females and pleasurable (or shameful) indulgences in sexual congress. Considering common aspects such as these requires looking at each at a high level: consider each behavior as a symbol.

At this high level we do not examine each culture. We also do not examine every unique personality of every Initiate. Enhancing and improving the Initiate, however, has proven to possess various common elements. These elements are the symbols and actions embodied by the the Luciferian Path. Think of this when confused or bewildered about certain practices! Choose parts of yourself – your present self or your ideal self- and relate them to these symbols! This is the heart – the grammar and structure- of Initiation.

The Way of the Adversary does not require submission to any god or belief structure. You choose which beliefs resonate with you. Each individual is, however, responsible *and accountable* to perpetually challenge each belief, reforming each as necessary. It is this method of perpetual challenge that is the Way of the Adversary.

Faith, when mentioned, refers to Faith in the Self. Such self-confidence is the bane of self-doubt and all counterproductive, self-destructive forces existing in the ego, psychology or spiritual essence of the individual.

Thought, word, and action are the building blocks creating mind and material existence. De-emphasize the thought, word and action. It is Creativity that is the essential fire that first enabled Lucifer the ability to rebel against heaven's cosmonopoly.

Imagination is the practice of creativity upon the mind. It is the suspension of restriction hindering one's perception. Unfolding Imagination is essential in overcoming any perceived limits of Self.

Doctrine, itself, refers not to some dogmatic practice required but the presentation and communication of a framework of symbols. This framework has a particular form and sequence which may be interpreted and activated per each individual's consideration.

All of this may be summarized by saying:
> *The Way of the Adversary is evidenced in these Luciferian doctrines and given impetus by Luciferian Faith. Impetus is born of Creativity measured by expansion of Imagination. Commensurate with the focus of the Practitioner, Self-Deification is achieved.*

This idea can be symbolically stated through the actions of Cain:
> *Lilith seduced Adam yet she refused to submit to him. Looking towards his mother's example, Cain slew Abel and, with the inspiration of the*

Archon Samael, embarked onto an unknown journey into the darkness that is the land of Nod.

Consider a statement made in a later chapter:

> *"The original union of Az and Satan came from the Devil falling into a deep slumber for three thousand years."*

A surface interpretation of the words might seem to indicate that a physical event of Az, a Zoroastrian demon(ness) was betrothed to the office of a Hebraic Adversary, Satan. Taken literally, one might be distracted by the truthfulness (or falsity) of the statement. However, the *symbol* of Az and the *attributes* of Satan illustrate a Mystery. An Initiate is charged with defining and activating the specific mysteries by exploring such symbols and attributes- those of Az and that of Satan - in a meaningful way to him- or herself.

Let us now look at another example from the myths of old. Cain first emerged as the Son of Samael. Samael, who had copulated with Eve, begot Cain, offspring of the Dragon. Lilith awakened Cain who had sacrificed his brother to feed his Daemon. This sacrifice as seen by Luciferians, again, as *at least* a symbol, or model, of casting off innocence, ignorance and weakness in exchange for wisdom and knowledge – they very chalice of the Gods!

Let us consider this short Luciferian poem:

> Tubal Cain became as in flesh a dragon
> In the nights when earth was young
> By the fierce red flame of his furnace black

> The strokes of his hammer sparked that within was called wise.
>
> And the red sparks lit the air, which was dedication to Azazyl

Here we see that the Forge, hammer and fire are mentioned, Let us think of this in terms of our own self – the Spirit as the forge, the hammer as the Art of Samael, and the fire is that of Samael and Lilith conjoined. Further analysis of the symbols in this text hints at even deeper meanings:

> Cain is sought in the hidden places of the earth, for he is the ancient and knows the unknown secrets of the earth. *So also might we seek the hidden.*

> Cain also appears as the wizened old man, robed and hooded who walks the path of old – oak ways within the fog. *So also might we reach into eternity while obscuring the sight of those choosing weakness.*

> He received the book of black art and the belt of the devil in shadowy rites. Cain thus became Witch – father: the forever-born of Azazel and Lilith. *So also might we be forever transformed through rites of rebellion, seduction and sorceries of darkness.*

This sorcerous path proves most challenging: it moves against the motions of natural order. It requires extreme amounts of self control to balance mind, body and spirit to successfully progress upon it. The Left Hand Path either envenoms/empowers or destroys/devoures.

This may be understood, as written by the ancient priests of Zoroaster, that he who practices the sorcery of the Dev becomes like the demon. Demon becomes Serpent. The sleeper awakens to weild the Great Lie.

Mysteries such as these abound in the works of the Luciferian Path. Look beyond the surface and forge your own way through the darkness. Create your symbols and design your attributes. While an inspiration to imagination, the Luciferian Path does not offer fantasy to escape this harsh reality. It is the whipping-way by which the strong shall tame the universe through intrigue, ambition, deceit and even annihilation, if need be. It is Self-Perfection and dominance measured by real results and achievement based on the parameters set by the Luciferian for him- or herself.

Arise, Magickian of Lucifer.

The Legion Within beckons.

MAGICKAL FOUNDATIONS

OBJECTIVES OF MAGICK

The activation of predatory instinct through magick is a distinguishing mark of the Luciferian Path. This is the prime method used by the Order of Phosphorus. Other ways to activate the Path include devotional practices such as prose, hymn and song. The Church of Adversarial Light is primarily focused on this form of work. This chapter focuses on magickal foundations necessary to understand, begin and sustain Luciferian initiatory practices.

No shortage of definitions for magick exist:

> *"Magick is the art of causing change internally and externally in accordance with the Will. Magick is the art of transformation into a sense of divine consciousness, thus it is meant to improve and assist the Luciferian."*
> -Michael W. Ford, The Bible of the Adversary

> *"Magick is the Science of understanding oneself and one's conditions. It is the Art of applying that understanding in action."*
> -Aleister Crowley, *Book IV*

> *"The change in situations or events in accordance with one's will, which would, using normally accepted methods, be unchangeable."*
> -Anton LaVey, *the Satanic Bible*

> *"Magic is but one's natural ability to attract without asking."*
> - A.O. Spare, *Logomachy of Zos*

Adding to these perceptions are the myriad forms of magick throughout diverse historical magickal cultures You are advised to study these in the "Legacy" appendix for more information.

The Left Hand Path defines a way of living and developing on this earth and in this life. It demands that you are accountabile for your own actions and the actions of everyone else impacting your life. Similarly, you are responsible for self-determined goals- and their accomplishment. Enjoying the pleasure of this world yet not falling prey to weakness is yet another challenge. The Initiate of the Left Hand Path invokes the Gods which represent the rebellious and strong aspects of the human personality – often societies' demons!

Lucifer is thus a perfect archetype for the Adversarial Path. Lucifer is the God of Light and Wisdom, yet incubates a dark or shadow side. Beneath the name of Lucifer you will find Samael, Satan, Ahriman, Set & Apep. There is also an equally strong Feminine aspect of the Adversary. In Sumerian Mythology TIAMAT, the primordial sea dragon, LILITH, the bride of Samael who was a Goddess of Sorcery, Vampires and the Night, HECATE, the Goddess of Witchcraft in ancient Greece are but a few.

High Black Magick and Low Black Magick are common practices in the Left Hand Path. The word 'Black' is described by Idries Shah as having the sound of FHM in the Arabic tongue. This equates it to a 'wise understanding'. Shah further notes that "Black" connects with hidden wisdom, hearkening a rallying cry of "Dar tariki, tariqat!"

In the Darkness, the Path.

The Left Hand Path is by universal perception as being the mutation or transformation of consciousness into a divinity or divine consciousness. The process of the practice of Magick and Sorcery is its method. These are the ways to propel the body-mind-soul towards higher levels of perception.

REASONS WHY MAGICK IS PRACTICED

1. To liberate yourself from restrictive beliefs you were brought up with. Better to plunge into darkness than to live in a shadow.
2. To examine deep set behaviors which may be causing problems, modify those behaviors and shape them into productive areas of your life. **Magickian, Renew Thyself.**
3. To open up spiritual communication and experience with the Luciferian current, i.e Gods, Daemon and Goddesses. It is irrelevant whether personal beliefs on whether these are sovereign beings, forces or just strains of psychological identification. All is interpreted by the Self. All begins within the Self. Magick extends you.
4. To build, strengthen and refine consciousness, which will in turn build personal Ego, confidence and charisma per one's own psychological make-up. **Every inner quality forged manifests exponentially in the external world.**
5. To define what is possible in your life when your mind is focused. Limits collapse as the imagination grows. **Magick purposefully binds the imagination to reality.**
6. Luciferians exalt life and celebrate both spiritual and the carnal aspects of it. One's focus may gravitate towards one or the other at any given moment or at different periods in a lifetime. The Luciferian Spirit reminds us to maintain a healthy balance. Symbiotically, the spiritual and the carnal are inherently connected. They feed upon each other. Full access to the glory flesh is not gained without sating

the spirit. Similarly, full access to the spirit is impossible without gorging the flesh.

7. Personal experience is paramount – don't assume something is so by word alone. Experience it. Challenge it. Affirm all things by your own standards; be careful that these standards do not lapse into stagnant restriction. Think of what you might do with the pinnacle of inspiration. Behold the perfect vision of your own cunning, creativity and life, manifest: the path of the Crooked Serpent begins.

MAGICKAL DYNAMICS

High Black Magick and Low Black Magick are common practices in the Left Hand Path. The word 'Black' is described by Idries Shah as having the sound of FHM in the Arabic tongue. This equates it to a 'wise understanding'. Shah further notes that "Black" connects with hidden wisdom, hearkening a rallying cry of "Dar tariki, tariqat!" In the Darkness, the Path.

Luciferian Magick heralds this use of Darkness. Its magickal objective is to Ascend and Become. Ascension is achieved by strengthening oneself through balanced doses of Willed Change. It is most easily understood by this simple formula:

$$Knowledge+Experience=Wisdom$$

Knowledge is gathered and then activated by experience. Results empower one with Wisdom. The Practitioner becomes more than he or she was previously. This is the essence of Ascension and Becoming.

Ascension may be realized through the magickal components of Will, Desire and Belief which make more sense when arranged sequentially:

Desire. The identification of wants or needs and the decision to act.
Belief. Inner reinforcement to propel one to obtain the Desire.
Will. Movement and active focus – real energy – expended to achieve Desire.

A successful magickal working has two key components:

Framework. A representation or construct of the desire. Imagination, exercised. The more physical and elaborate the construct, the better. Frameworks are placeholders

for Belief. It may include the altar, tools, candles and the ritual performance itself.
Energy. Energy inhabits the Framework. It is propulsion of Will by Belief. It imprints reality. The act of imprinting. Magickal power.

These components can be considered in contrabst. Energy without a Framework is self-indulgent fantasy to no great end. Framework without Energy is dead ritual.

Methods of applying energy to framework include stabbing dolls with pins, the Death Posture, bleeding upon sigils and various sympathetic actions. Each involves investing a framework with energy. Other methods include Luciferian Yoga, meditation, martial arts. Flood or starve the senses. Confound the hierarchy of needs. Suspension of Desire allows the whole mind – conscious, subconscious, unconscious – to take free reign in saturating Framework with Energy.

<u>Whatever the method, ordinary consciousness must be interrupted.</u> Energy must flow.

Interior forces, ancient frameworks, the primal energies of beast and monster, the subjugation and assumption of other-person or other-world energy: these are all aspects of the Luciferian Path. Whatever form, reinforcement is the final ingredient of Luciferian Magick. If the act seems to fail, improve the framework. Practice forms of raising/manipulating/stealing energy. Perform the enhanced rite. Improve, enhance, and repeat until successful. Such contextual failure serves you by offering an opportunity to enhance your magickal stature.

Be prepared; attaining proficiency takes great time and develops at considerable expense.

Emphasis on Imagination is frequent and significant: it is the first action in a sequence of actions vital to magick.

Cain's heart was driven by the imagination in his mind before smashing the head of his brother. Adam's seduction by Lilith was an abominable, deliberate process. Such transformations are imagined before manifesting. Or are they?

A true Black Initiation is experiencing something beyond the limitations of Imagination. Direct contact with the Lord of Self is the gateway to initiation. Everything changes. Initiation is Great Change. The Night reveals the Hidden to all of us,

In this way and by this merit that we denizens of the Adversary ascend into Darkness. We go without trepidation, without fear, without regret. We do not rely on opposites to define us – only our own dictates and movements. We ascertain, transcend, conquer and bleed our self-forged core into the furthest reaches of the indefinable. This is the Left Hand Path.

Embrace it as a wolf or keep it hidden as frightened sheep.

ADVERSARIAL PANTHEONS

Many gods, goddesses, demons and angels are indexed and expounded upon in manuscripts of the Luciferian Path. Understanding the nature of these beings can be daunting, even confusing. This section explores deific masks, the significance of the Adversary to the Luciferian Path. A concentrated table of attributes examining key figures in this Path is also provided as a quick reference.

Understand that the concepts herein are provided as a rational model of Luciferian Pantheons. Your experience, imagination and manifestation as a result of these may lead you to different belief systems and models. This is perfectly understood and even encouraged! Take this model as one example and not any sort of dogmatic assertion. Beginners may find the model useful as a starting point in their magickal practices.

DEIFIC MASKS OF THE ADVERSARY

Outside our perceptions of space and time – beyond concepts of cohesion and sequence – exists vast stirrings of raw power. This power may be canopied under the name of Primordial Darkness. It is cohesive yet it is oblivious to human concepts of individual sovereignty or patronage. It is multiplicitous. No macrocosmic sense of duality or contrast may be found – such power is endless, eternal and unbound.

Within this canopy of Primal Darkness is constant-shuffling, boiling chaos. Systems and forms both emerge and collapse within it. Collapse denotes the lack of human context as a means to measure or discern its attributes. Emergence denotes at least some synergy with human perception. This synergy can be named as a deity.

Emergence in the context of ritual requires the Initiate to identify and sanctify those parts of self corresponding with the deity or deities selected. This is a deific mask.

It is the challenge of the Initiate to draw these forces from within, without and around. This process is explained in the ritual chapters of this book.

Such deities enter our awareness by binding a mask of chaos to a part of the Initiate and/or his altar and tools and the ritual practiced. Identify attributes from Witch Moon, Luciferian Witchcraft, Bible of the Adversary, or any of the

works of the Luciferian Path. Take these attributes and qualify them by asking basic questions such as:
1. Who from the presented pantheons is applicable to the working?
2. What attributes are historical? Mythological? Diabolical?
3. How does this deity relate to others in the pantheons presented?

Take the answers to these questions and configure your rite accordingly. Once the god or goddess makes itself known to you, either by willed ritual results, symbolic representation, inner vision or even physical manifestation, you have successfully activated a Deific Mask.

The magickian's right to tap these forces is by the existence – and activation – of his or her creative will. It may be appropriate to be commanding, seductive, conniving, forthright. This is left to the Initiate's discretion.

THE LUCIFERIAN

At the center of the Luciferian Pantheon is the Luciferian. Luciferian Magick is more than the improvement self-esteem by repetitive ritual affirmations. Understanding Luciferian ideology – what it is and what it is not – is a first step to realizing the forms and practices of this path.

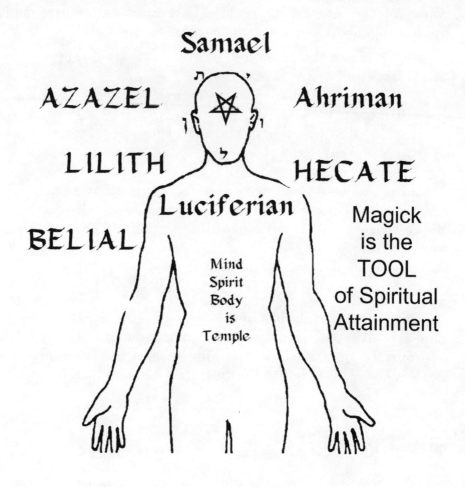

Above: The Self is the Central Focus as a Luciferian.

The Right Hand Path, Christianity, Buddhism, Islam glorify a God outside of the self – a "good" being which has fathered the human spirit, who wants to escape the flesh to join the heaven or bliss elsewhere.

Understand this in contrast to the Left Hand Path of the Luciferian:

A Luciferian possesses a cradled arrogance of spirit while remaining focused and alert.

A Luciferian becomes a living embodiment of Spirit, thus e body is a temple. Do not defile it in any way that might inhibit your metamorphosis unless the reward outweighs the risk.

A Luciferian recognizes Magick is a tool to master this world and to open a gateway to the beyond. Deeply spiritual and certain of physically death, the Luciferian aims for a continued spiritual existence beyond the flesh and grave through magickal means

A Luciferian is of the fire which is illuminated from clay. Aggression, born of weakness. Light emerging from darkness. As stated in the Bible of the Adversary, all magick is black.

While black, the Luciferian's magick is not inherently malelfic or negative. It holds closer association to KHEM, the root-meaning of the word black. It self-awakens and rewards isolation with unnatural gifts. It is inclusive of dualities: positive and negative, constructive and destructive, aggressive and receptive. It also moves beyond duality into polarities, propagating both opposite aspects from a single source: Self.

A Luciferian views this world as something to possess, something to enjoy and to use as a means to gain Wisdom and Strength - here and now!

Black Magic, as such, then springs from a well with no center- and no periphery. It is a wellspring of knowledge. It holds every potential and every power that could conceivably manifest. Every endearing embrace. Every horrific murder.

HUMAN MASKS OF THE ADVERSARY

Magickians today face more rigorous challenges than in any age previous. Self-Perfection manifests in one's effectiveness in both internal and external worlds. Mastering diversified roles is one way to bring about such perfection. Such human masks of the Luciferian masks include:

The Artist. Relates to the focus of power within the construct of beauty and revulsion. This could be through music, sculpture, drawing, painting. All of these contribute to becoming a master of rite-craft.

The Scholar. The study of ancient and modern magicks provides one with limitless sources of knowledge. This knowledge translates into diversified experiences and empowerment.

The Philosopher. Always question; never stagnate.

The Hermit. Recognizing the benefits of periodic hibernation and the opportunities in character development according to Self – not social constructs.

The Athlete. Overcoming physical limitations assists the magickian in mental endurance through practices such as Luciferian Yoga. What better way to express Self-sanctification!

The Statesman. Listening, interjection, negotiation and self-promotion are all excellent tactics in the masterful execution of Will.

The Provider. Attend needs of blood- and witch- kin alike. It is much more efficient to sustain a powerbase among those giving willing consent to your authority.

The Example. Create an example by which others will hunger and attempt to mimic New souls may be called to

Darkness just as cunning serpent spurred Adam and Eve in the primordial garden.

The Agent. Acts of seeming generosity inspire loyalty and grant you control over the perceptions of others. As a power-broker, one becomes the face of the powers there trafficked and, ultimately, that power.

The Mortician. The absence of fear is Exhausted capability is the absence of fear: further your life by the wielding of death.

The Deity. The rejection of total submission to anything or anyone is key to magickal longevity in the Luciferian Path. Never submit to another person or one's base or aesthetic drives if that submission unacceptably decreases one's power.

The Whore. Balancing the scales of seduction, hedonism, risk and reward to further opportunity as one worships sacred desire and possession and expiration.

The Assassin. The art of silence and subterfuge.

The Predator. The hunt concluding in possession and devourment of the unfortunate prey

All these roles constitute parts of the psyche that must be mastered. This is not a complete list; just a precursory one. An in-depth study of the Luciferian Tarot is an exhaustive exercise.

GODS AND GODDESSES

"This is not a path of prayer and supplication, but recognition of the sorcerer's own inherent powers. The forces of Darkness are called upon as a means of self-expression, self-empowerment, and self-deification." – Nathaniel Harris, (author of WITCHA- A Book of Cunning, Mandrake of Oxford, and current Magister of The Red Circle, England) from the Introduction to "Luciferian Witchcraft" by Michael W. Ford

The God of Luciferian Witchcraft is Seth-an, or Set (the same as Samael, Satan). This is the Egyptian Prince of Darkness, a Lord of Chaos and sorcerous power. Set should not be considered merely a God in an anthropomorphic sense, rather a deific force which is the very essence of our being. When Azazel or Lucifer brought to Cain the Black Flame of Consciousness, this was as too Set's gift to mankind. By working in the circles of Luciferian Craft, you are merely fulfilling your ancient heritage. While some choose paths less dangerous than this; the reality of witchcraft as a Luciferian Gnosis cannot be denied. The Great Work in reference to Set is for the magician to seek divinity, which is awareness, individuality and personal power. By believing in yourself rather than something 'higher' than you (The only Higher Angelick or Demonic being is YOU, the Luciferic Angel or Holy Guardian Angel) you become as your models.

Within the Black Tradition the Luciferian Trinity which is composed of Samael – Lilith – Cain hold significance in the model of practice within the cult. This Trinity is an alchemical process of becoming in which the magician aligns and utilizes the deific associations of Samael – Lilith – Cain to transform their consciousness into the divine essence which is Baphomet, the Head of Knowledge. To described Samael, a small section as follows is from LIBER HVHI, a ritual work which defines the deeper and darker practice of the Left Hand Path in terms of Witchcraft.

"For the Devil is called Diabolus, that is, flowing downwards: that he which swelled with pride, determined to reign in high places, fell flowing downwards to the lowest parts, like the torrent of a violent stream." –The Fourth Book of Occult Philosophy

"It is written in the Bible that Samael/Satan fell from heaven as lightening, being a flash downwards, who before the fall, was a guarding Seraph around the throne of God. After his fall he was a master of death, the very poison of God yet he was also a Giver of Life, being the father between fallen angel and woman. In later Jewish writings, Samael is associated with the name Malkira, which Morris Jastrow Jr. associated with Malik-Ra, being "The Evil Angel" and the name Matanbuchus, being a form of Angro-Mainyush or Ahriman. Here does the circle become closed and the nature of the First Angel become perceived or sensed. In ongoing ritual work, the magician begins identifying his or herself with Samael (and Lilith) within the parameters of their own life and initiation.

The Lord of the Earth, being a name ascribed to Samael (Satan) and his fallen angels and demons, are but considered astral spirits, that which no longer take physical form, but may become manifest through the magician or witch who may make a "pact" with them, being initiation and dedication to the Left Hand Path. Samael is the patron spirit of the Left Hand Path, as his Word is what formed our thoughts and gave us the inner fire of the Black Flame, our individual process of thought and free will. The magicians who aligned their will with the Left Way, that of Samael (the Devil), were given powers over the earth in one way or another; all the while strengthening, defining and expanding their conscious. In Exodus 7 the magicians were able to make frogs and serpents by the power they obtained in the Devil, thus such creatures are astral forms of Ahriman (Samael) and the dreaming body of witches and sorcerers." -Liber HVHI

Godforms hold specific power within the cults of witchcraft as what is empowered from the practitioner themselves. The Gods and Goddesses would not exist in any tangible form if humanity did not empower them; either subconsciously or consciously, thus by the Adept becoming does the Godform become. Deific energy is a source not only based within the blood of the practitioner, of the atavistic or primal recesses of the human mind. This Deific energy or power may be recalled into the flesh and conscious mind of the practitioner, thus one finds the knowledge undertaken by earlier sects such as The Golden Dawn, the Maskhara of the Arabic and Asian tribes, Austin Osman Spare's Zos Kia Cultus, etc. There are numerous rituals explored by Luciferian Sabbat practitioners within The Order of Phosphorus and the Black Order of the Dragon which utilize old methods of lycanthropy and the 'shedding of flesh', of shape shifting by dream in Therion form to go forth to the erotic convulsions of the Infernal Sabbat.

The Goddess of Luciferian Witchcraft is Lilith or Babalon, as described previously. She is also Hecate, the Darkened Moon Goddess of the Cunning Circle, whose blessing is both youth, imagination and death. The Son is within you and that is Cain, the Baphometic Daemon whose magick is the core essence of the religion of sorcery. The very circle casting rite as written by Gerald Gardner presents the Mother of Witchcraft, "Mother, Darksome and Divine, Mine the Scourge and Mine the Kiss, The Five-point Star of Love and Bliss". Within the circle there is the very Graal of the Adversary, that through Self-Love can the essence of the Pentagram be sensed and understood. He refers to Hecate or Lilith (via Diana) as being "Hell's dark mistress, Heaven's Queen." This is the dual nature of the Devil and his Bride, the Adversary. That by both Sabbat rites does the cup of Heaven (Aethyr, Luciferian Sabbat) and Hell (Infernal, Chthonic Sabbat) are filled.

The most important figure which not only inspired Ahriman, but empowered him was the whore Jeh or Az. In Manichaean religious lore, Az is considered the Great Whore who played a very important role to her mate, Ahriman. In Manichaean traditions Az was a spirit which made he home in the caves and dark places of the earth, as well as Hell. Az was considered to have taught demons and arch-fiends how to copulate and act in lewd ways, later teaching the Fallen Angels how to excite themselves and others sexually. Az used her sorceries to produce Dragon-children and to then create other demons and daughters who were of her own blood. Az was known to have devoured her children and their children, then create more to later devour them as well.

"And he kissed Jeh upon the head, and the pollution which they call menstruation became apparent in Jeh" – The Bundahishn, translated by E. W. West

Az (also known as Jeh) as the demon of death, called Concupiscence, is considered in many points to be the instinctual side of man. R.C. Zaehner describes Az has having a three – fold nature, consisting of eating, sexual desire and yearning for whatever she comes across by her senses. The nature of Az is also considered to be *'disorderly motion[1]'* which makes reference to counter clockwise movement, chaos and antinomianism. Zaehner writes that-

"The demon Az is a Buddhist rather than a Zoroastrian idea; there is no trace of it in the Avesta. In Buddhism, on the other hand, the root cause of the chain of conditioned existence is avidya, 'ignorance', and its principle manifestation is trshna, 'thirst', which means the desire for continued existence."

Furthermore, Az represents the ideal and concept of self-deification through a Willed existence, that the *trshna* concept is one of vampirism and desire. Thus Az represents the Left Hand Path as a rite of passage of becoming. Continued existence is essentially the survival of the psyche or essential self; there is no union with the natural order that which can eliminate the mind. The practitioner does not seek

---

[1] This word can be related to Anticlockwise movement, or Widdershins.

to join with it; rather he or she seeks to remain separate from it in their own self-created subjective world.

As with the Manichaeans, Az is the "Mother of All Demons", thus a powerful hidden Light behind Ahriman. As the Devil's Bride she inspires and equally commands her presence, manifests her Will and accomplishes that which other demons could not. Ahriman was taken with her.

Az within Zoroastrianism is not by any mentionable gender, but Ahriman's assistant if you will is called in the Pahlavi books called Jeh, which means roughly 'whore'. She would corrupt or rather awaken mankind and womankind to debauchery and sexual pleasure.

Theodore bar Konai[2] described an interesting tale of Ahriman and his sway that he held with women:

"After Ohrmazd had given women to righteous men, they fled and went over to Satan; and when Ohrmazd provided righteous men with peace and happiness, Satan provided women too with happiness. As Satan had allowed the women to ask for anything they wanted, Ohrmazd feared they might ask to have intercourse with the righteous men and that these might suffer damage thereby. Seeking to avoid this, he created the god Narseh (a youth) of fifteen years of age. And he put him, naked as he was behind Satan so that the women should see him, desire him and ask Satan for him. The women lifted their hands up towards Satan and said: "Satan, our father, give us the god Narseh as a gift."

The original union of Az and Satan came from the Devil falling into a deep slumber for three thousand years. Unconscious, Ahriman would not awaken for any reason. Numerous demons and shadows tried to awaken Ahriman by telling of their deeds, nothing would stir him to

---
[2] See R.C. Zaehner, The Dawn and Twilight of Zoroastrianism New York, NY 1961

consciousness. After three thousand years the Whore came unto Ahriman and said to him-

"Arise O our Father, for in the battle to come I shall let loose so much affliction on the Rightcous Man and the toiling Bull that, because of my deeds, they will not be fit to live. I shall take away their dignity, I shall afflict the water, I shall afflict the earth, I shall afflict the fire, I shall afflict the plants, I shall afflict all the creation which Ohrmazd has created."

Here we see that Az has knowledge and control over the elements and that which the Natural Order observes as correct. She wishes to change it according to Her will, to afflict is to darken its essence with much of the Light she was endowed with early on.

Cain was the Son born of by some accounts Samael (the Devil) and Lilith (through Eve), the first Satanist and Witch.

"It is said within the dark traditions that the Bible is mistaken with regards to Cain's true parentage. Cain was in fact a half human, half demon bastard child of Adam and Lilith. It was for this reason that the Lord would not accept his offerings and prayers, rather than any specific demands of animal sacrifice. The tale continues with Cain being cursed to wander the earth as a vagabond, with the ground he tills never giving bounty." – Nathaniel J. Harris, The Mark of Cain, the First Satanist and First Murder.

In certain rabbinical literature, the Daughters of Cain were those who joined in sexual union with the Fallen Angels, the Watchers, and gave birth to the Nephilim, the Giants who were war like and brutal. They were said to have populated the earth in plenty, and attacked the children of Seth. In Manichaean lore, the Queen of Demons and spiritual initiator of Cain, Lilith – Az, taught the fallen angels to form physical bodies and join with others sexually. It is suggested also by writers Kaufmann Kohler, W.H. Bennett and Louis Ginzberg that the Children of Cain spent their days at the foot of a mountain (Eden?) practicing in wild orgies with the music of Lucifer through that created by Jubal.

Women, the first Pairikas or Faeries/Witches, in their beautiful appearances, invited the sons of Seth (children of god) and copulated with them, bearing other children. This Jewish Folklore presents the earliest forms of the Witches Sabbat as a Luciferian celebration and practice of sexual magick.

"To Philo, likewise, Cain is the type of avarice, of "folly and impiety" ("De Cherubim," xx.), and of self-love ("De Sacrificiis Abelis et Caini"; "Quod Deterius Potiori Insidiari Soleat," 10). "He built a city" (Gen. iv. 17) means that "he built a doctrinal system of law-lessness, insolence, and immoderate indulgence in pleasure" ("De Posteritate," 15); and the Epicurean philosophers are of the school of Cain, "claiming to have Cain as teacher and guide, who recommended the worship of the sensual powers in preference to the powers above, and who practiced his doctrine by destroying Abel, the expounder of the opposite doctrine" (ib. 11)." – The Jewish Encyclopedia, compiled by Kaufmann Kohler, W. H. Bennett, Louis Ginzberg

Herein we can see that Cain is thus a flesh and blood embodiment of the Luciferian Path itself, he is the Son of Satan and Lilith, the dark essence which is deeply connected with Eve, the wife of Adam. Cain is not only the patron father of Witches, also the symbol of the initiate upon the antinomian path.

The suggestions of the foundation of sorcery and cunning craft is from the earliest legends, memories and mythology of mankind. Cain who wandered east to the Land of Nod became essentially, according to the "truth of the circle" the first Satanist and Witch, whose children beget children and the blood line of the cunning were born. It is suggested in some Jewish lore that the daughters of Cain were the ones to seduce or copulate with the fallen angels, the Watchers.

It is beginning with the Watchers that the balanced aspects of Angelic and Satanic Magick are found – it is the very atavistic depths in which this bloodline still rests deep within our psyche, along with the serpents and Therion-Atavisms within our flesh. "The Book of Enoch", translated from the Ethiopian by R.H. Charles, in the 69th Chapter, presents the names and therein sorcerous essence of the Luciferian Angels, who are the very foundation of the Arte of Magick.

The mentioned Watchers who descended again to earth were: Samjaza, Artaqifa, Armen, Kokabel, Turael, Rumjal, Danjal, Neqael, Baraqel, Armaros, Batarjal, Busasejal, Hananel, Turel, Simapesiel, Tumael, Turel, Rumael, and Azazel. These are among the names of the Chiefs of the Watchers who came into flesh upon the earth.

Jeqon led the others to earth to begin to lust for the daughters of Cain. Asbeel was said to have given evil council to the Sons of God, being the Watchers, that they should go forth and copulate with the daughters of Cain.

Gadreel taught unto man, woman and child the blows of death and creation of armor and weapons. Penemue taught unto the wise the art of ink and writing, as well as the bitter and the sweet, good and evil. This is the spirit who gave unto the Cunning the Book of Arte, which brought forth both Demon and Angel, those hidden Therionick Forms of Darkness-made-flesh, the art of lycanthropy.

Kasdeja taught men the art of working with demons and spirits, as well as abortions and the Secret art of the Noon tide Serpent, Tabaet. The Angelick spirit Kasbeel was the bringer of the Oath, when he was with the heavens, his name was known as Biqa.

CONCEPTS OF INITIATION

Initiation is a step on the path of the Adversary, to begin a journey on the scales and shields of the Crooked Serpent, Leviathan. The following ritual, CASTING THE SHADOW OF CAIN is a powerful rite which acts as a "Crossing of the Threshold". Initiation is the first steps into the path of Lucifer, one of hidden wisdom and the knowledge of self. By knowing who you are, strengths, weakness and what you want to become does the path of darkness reveal light. The light is wisdom. Magick is a tool which opens the mind to the unknown. With knowledge of the unknown comes power. Luciferians thirst for power. We want to control our lives, our possibilities in life and death.

Initiation into the Luciferian Mysteries is one which requires someone who is able to seek mysteries to discover knowledge; you must embrace the darkness as a part of yourself, understanding that the abyss is an endless fountain of power.

The highest aim of many initiatory orders is to thrust the candidate into the abyss, destroying the human ego and hence creating a being of light who is merely a vessel for some imbalanced god. Our Luciferian tradition, in contrasts, sponsors an abysmal plunge on the very outset. The goal is not to dissolve the ego but to ignite it. Once lit, the Initiate empowers self and addresses any human weakness to emerge as a beacon of his own light.

Begin your path as a Luciferian knowing you will be challenged and tested. Through this magickal path you shall ascended as a God or Goddess. You develop yourself in the archetypical image of the Adversary.

Through the Mask of the isolated one, the wanderer who first spilled blood to sacrifice to his demon, whose mark was that of initiation, can the path of light be seen. That the first murderer destroyed the weakness of his own self to descend into darkness and then again into light presents a model of initiation. It is more than a mere model to some, rather a living spirit which inspires the self; acts as a muse and elevates the self to higher levels of perception.

The Faith of Cain is the faith of the self; antinomianism and passing beyond all borders. The nature of the Father of Cain, being Satan/Samael, is to be as the Adversary, to test the self and the others, by chaos can order then be truly born. As with Order being born, thus it must die and chaos must bring a needed change. Do not mistake Order for progressive action; as Chaos is the only law of certain un-law.

Cain is the point of continual transformation, this process of initiatory symbolism is best understood as the following:

Transformation	Process	Deific Mask
Clay	Uninitiated	Abel
Fire	Forge	Cain
Light	Awakened	Lucifer-Azazel

The symbolism of Cain and Lucifer-Azazel (Azal'ucel) is the process of self-illuminating initiation: a self-directed achievement.

The aim of the magician is to become like Lucifer, the struggle against the Natural Order which denies the will to become isolate and unique, to fight against the absolute or AinSoph which would devour consciousness – it is light merciless, thoughtless, uncaring. This AinSoph as the Cabalists call it is the perception of unity with the limitless light, God or the Kether of the Tree of Life. Before one may approach this light, the Luciferian Spark within must be kindled. The magician must fight to develop the self from the identity to being lost in some vague universal oneness.

THE SHADOW or WITCH NAME

As I was called "The Night Ravener" by a Sabbatic intiate in the late 1990's, the importance of names in magical rites is significant. During such workings, you may hear your name of darkness or shadow whispered in dreams – it represents your true nature. Chose your name carefully, it must appeal to you above all and represent part of who you are. A part that will dominate. As you gain experience upon the path, your title may change to represent your current area of initiation. Some choose to keep the same name.

THE BOOK

The Magical record is a very important book – it is a blank tome which you will keep daily record of your workings. Why would this be important? It will be a future guide to what you have had results with – and what did not work. You will begin to see patterns, when you work strongest and when you are less effective. Imagine what you could do for yourself with such information!

THE CIRCLE CASTING RITUAL

"The Circle within Luciferian Witchcraft represents the very binding space of the sorcerers body, both of spirit/celestial and flesh/infernal. It is the symbol of both the Sun and the Moon, the sphere which begets strength and the very focus of the Magician." ADAMU

The circle casting ritual in Luciferian Magick is based around not banishing, however asserting power and raising the spirit to specific points of power. The circle represents the Body of the Luciferian, when you are within the circle you announce and focus your desire on the task at hand. Once you get very proficient at this basic casting ritual, you may wish to move on to one of the rites from THE BIBLE OF THE ADVERSARY.

WIDDERSHINS

Widdershins are movements around the circle in an anti clockwise dance. Some witches may find it useful to recite the Lord's Prayer Backwards while moving widdershins in the beginning of the Sabbat Rite, this allowing or 'giving permission' to the nature of the Working itself.

CASTING THE SHADOW OF CAIN
A Ritual of Initiation

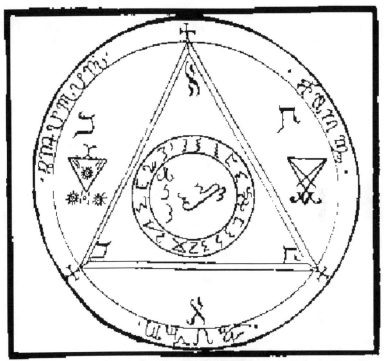

Point the tip of the triangle to the North
Sacred to Cain
The Magickian stands in the circle of Lucifer
the center affirming the union of the Daemon and Man

One of the early Luciferian rites based on the casting of the circle, this small ritual was designed to imbibe the sorcerer with a focused current of being, a dedication to the path of Cainnite Antinomianism. One may use the Grand Luciferian Circle as a means of Self-Deification, the Immolation of the Spirit by assuming the mask of the Witch-Begetter, Cain the Blacksmith.

Using a cloth large enough to stand within, paint the image of the Grand Luciferian Circle. You will want to point the tip of the Triangle towards the North, as this is sacred to Cain.

Your altar may face North, the direction sacred to Cain, Ahriman and Lilith.

Light Three candles upon the altar, red in the center, Black on each side. This represents the Luciferian Trinity – Samael – Lilith – Cain.

Using the Athame, hold it up and recite facing the North:

> *"I call forth the infernal shadows which nourish my body and soul;*
>
> *I invoke the circle which empowers my form of being,*
>
> *From the North, I invoke the force of Cain[3], being my shadow of self*
>
> *Let the Blackened Flame illuminate from this very Forge!*
>
> *From the West, I invoke the force of Anubis, the Opener of the Way*
>
> *Let the Violet Light of the Dead empower my Spirit!*
>
> *From the South, I invoke the force of Thoth, whose lamp illuminates my path*
>
> *Let the Fires of Wisdom and Self-Discover Guide my path!*
>
> *From the East, I invoke Set, being the fire and strength of spirit*
>
> *Reveal thy essence as Azal'ucel, the Fiery Djinn of Change and Rebellion!*

---

[3] Originally, Set was placed towards the North. The Egyptian symbolism here is a beginning Mask for something deeper, traditional Daemonology is utilized in further workings.

Face the North, pointing the Athame in this direction:

> *Cain, bringer of the cauldron of change and self transformation do protect my very being of self, that I may grow and ascend in our family born of Witch Blood pure.*
>
> *I seek the coils of Leviathan, The Darkened Grave earth of Ahriman and the Dream plane of Lucifer. Allow the gates to open before me!"*
>
> *I encircle myself in the Dragon's coils; the Beast of my father arises within!*
>
> *I hold the Skull of Abel, being the vessel of my Familiar!*
>
> *I hold the Hammer of the Forge, which I spark the Cunning Fire of Becoming!*
>
> *My eyes hold the desert tales of ages forgotten; while my flesh fades my spirit is immortal!*
>
> *I wear the crimson caul of my mother, Lilith, who speaks with me through dreams!*
>
> *I carry the serpent's skin of Azal'ucel, my Holy Spirit!*
>
> *I am Cain, loner and Witch Soul of the Immortal Fire!*
>
> *So it is done!*

THE RITUAL OF SUMMONING CAIN

Using the Grand Luciferian Circle, light one single black flame in the center of the altar. You may wish to have a symbol of Cain or Baphomet at the head of the altar.

Using an Athame, hold the blade facing the North, visualize the image of Cain and as you recite imagine your own body becoming the mirror-image of Cain. The essence of this ritual is to affirim that YOU are the first and last, Azothoz, of Alpha and Omega, the ONLY God that is. The aim of this is to lay a foundation that the Magickian is accountable alone for his or her own sorcerous path. Have a chalice filled with liquid to drink from, symbolic of the blood of Abel.

LIGHTING THE BLACK CANDLE, HOLD THE BLADE TOWARD THE ALTAR:

In the Circle of Cain does the Devil take flesh

By the hammer, skull-fetish and forked stave does thy Will announce

Weave thy magick in the Sun and the Moon, both shadows shall cast

With thy bride are Dragon-Children Born

When Lilith spreads her bloodstained legs

THE LORD'S PRAYER REVERSED

(phonetically)

Nema! Livee morf su revilled tub
Noishaytpmet ootni ton suh deel
Suh tshaiga sapsert tath yeth
Vigrawf eu za sesapsert rua suh vigrawf.
Derb ilaid rua yed sith suh vig
Neveh ni si za thre ni
Nud eeb liw eyth
Muck mod-ngik eyth
Main eyth eeb dwohlah
Neveh ni tra chioo
Rertharf rua!

O' Cain, spirit born of fire and darkness, shadowed initiator!

O' Cain, who wanders the earth from deserts to forests –

Brought forth from the womb, flesh-born son of the Dragon and the Harlot Goddess, mother of Witch Blood.

Spirit and Lord of the Blackened Fires of the Forge, who tasted the blood mark as an X upon the brow, whose mark is also the darkened ink of the well of the Peacocks scribe.

O' Cain, who was awakened by the Skull bearing Omen of Abel –

Lord of Beasts and initiator of sorcerous fire, werewolf – shapeshifter!

Let me see within and beyond the Caul of Lilith's veil!

Father and brother of the caves wherein are ancient shades,

Who hold the book of dreaming which is the primal word of the serpent-

Cain, Lord of Beasts and transformation, I summon thee, invocate thee within –

Shall your lightening strike upon the forge and illuminate my spirit!

Take your left hand; mark an "X" for the crossroads on your forehead. You may do such in your own blood if you wish.

'I deny God and all Religion

I curse, blaspheme, and provoke God with all despite

I give my faith to the Devel, and my worship and offer sacrifice to him

I do solemnly vow and promise all my progeny unto the Devel

I swear to the Devel to bring as many into his society as I can

I will always swear in the name of the Devel. [4]

My brow marked in blood, horned walker of worlds!

Strike now with thy hammer, shall the Eye of the Serpent open forth!

Unveiled in the Nightside do I come forth!

That I walk the path of Dragon born,

---

[4] A historical witchcraft initiation verse – the invocation of the Adversary.

Caster of the first circle of emerald and crimson flame.

Gatekeeper and Horned shape shifter – open forth the fiery path!

Illuminate the blackened flame!

Shall I awake the serpent born in the Devil's Skin – CAIN I SUMMON THEE!

The Formula of the Embodiment of Cain

Tubal - Cain, horned lord and first of witches blood
O Cain, who with the hands of the devil do bless
The bone charms under the moon
Nomadic daemon that as first born is illuminated
With the fire of Shaitan, thy father
From the forge does the spark fly
Those who dream unto thy path may become through it
Thy bloodletter, which struck the flesh clay of Abel
Is blessed with the blood dripping kiss of the serpent's tongue
The skull in thy hands a place of dwelling
From where the shades of the tomb do gather
In the devil's name I conjure thee
Cain, Qayin
From the deserts, from the forests, shall I become in your name...
I drink in honor of the Horned One
I drink the blood of Abel
I become as the Beast on earth
Hail thou self, O Cain awakened!
Drink from chalice, end ritual.

TIAMAT - The Rite of Self Creation

Initiation Ritual 2

The aim of self-creation is to continually evolve, mutate and become something better. This ritual is a Mass of Tiamat, holding a gateway to her abyss as the primal form of Lilith. Tiamat or Azhdeha is Lilith in her most primal and draconian form; the very possibility of her manifestation and a circle of deific power for those who may have the mind and courage to tap this source.

INSTRUCTIONS:

Let the magician adorn his or her chamber with images of the Primal mother – Tiamat, the Dragon, the constellation of Draco, the very place of her being in the stars. A chalice filled with the appropriate elixir representing the waters of the abyss, the very matter which is formed by the fire of the spirit. Let the Athame be the dagger which is used to Will the mind to self-creation.

Cast your circle (SHADOW OF CAIN) as you are the center of time, each quarter being an expansion of your Being and thus your Will.

HOLD THE ATHAME TO THE ALTAR:

"Awake Azazel, fire spirit who brings the knowledge of weapons and defense!

Awake Gadrel, who knows of death as initiation and the form of the serpent, whose knowledge of the instruments of death shall be our gift and knowledge!

Awake Kasyade, who has knowledge of the fallen ones, of shades and demons, whose art of encircling lives on through us!

Awake Penemue, who has knowledge of the bitterness and sweetness and how to use the world to manifest desire!

Awaken Great Serpent Tabaet, who has knowledge of the ancient waters!

HOLD THE ATHAME FACING THE IMAGE OF TIAMAT:

Mummu Hubur, stir and arise, awake in the darkness, awake in the abyss

She is who is terrible to face, she who devours and swallows up life

She who brings life to those who may face her, Mummu Hubur, begetter of dragons

I come forth to you, as lover, as your son, Stir up O Dragon Goddess

I am restless day and night, I seek to become and form the darkness into matter

With the flame given by my Father, I summon thee, I am of the Blood of Qingu, I am the Kin of this Flame"

HOLD THE DAGGER FACING THE IMAGE OF TIAMAT

Within me, charge my blood to turn as poison, nectar to the wise

Breed within me black serpents, sharp of tooth and merciless of fang

I shall be the un faceable weapon, fill my body with venom

I shall become as a ferocious dragon, cloaked in the fearsome rays of your sight

I am creating my Deific being from thee, with this Blade I cut weakness and emerge Godlike, I shall bring your children into this world!

Whoever shall look upon me shall collapse in utter terror"
(9X)

My body shall rise up continually and never turn away from my challenges!

I summon thee, Mush-Hushshu Dragon, Lahmu, Horned Serpent, Ugallu Demon, serpent man, rabid dog, bull man, empower me with merciless weapons, manifest my desire.

Mummu Tiamat, envenom me as Night, illuminate me in the fiery day, Cast thy spell upon me for I shall be as Qingu, my father – the Greatest in the Gods' Assembly.

I shall form my will and desire from the forgotten darkness, as thy Son and Lover, Mummu Hubar, arise in me, empower me!

Salamu Tammabukku, Elu, mush, mush, Elu, Nekelmu Ina

(Black Dragon Raise Up, Serpent, Serpent, Raise up, Evil Eye within)

Salamu Kishpu Ina, mush elu, mummu tiamat elu

(Black Sorcery Within, Serpent Raise up, Mother Tiamat raise up)

I drink now the primal waters, the abyssic darkness

Drink from the Chalice and visualize your spirit transforming into the image of a dragon.

With my body I shall form my desire, become the Lord of the Circle

So it shall be!"

THE LUCIFERIAN SUPPER OF CAIN

The practitioners should have some meat, prepared medium rare or even rare to consume symbolic of the Flesh of Abel. The witches will also need to have some wine or ale symbolic of the Blood of Abel. If vegan, improvise.

The altar may feature the Black flame, other candles may burn as well. You may have a black mirror near the altar or hanging, it is meaningful to stare into as you invoke – it relates back to the self.

The cup used in the ritual would be your traditional chalice, or even opportunity presents itself – a Kapala or skull cap.

DAGGER SHOULD BE RAISED UP
Recite:

"I am that which first caressed stone with the flesh of Abel

Whose last breath sucked at life as fangs on a vagina sucking at the feverish cock of a fallen priest, a church painted black with the blood of the moon.

The falling rock tore away the ignorance of Cain, who was no longer as Abel, when the blade tore into flesh the flies heard this delicate call

Like the sound of leather stretching, and a skull cracking open as a cock being withdrawn from the moment of ejaculation upon a whores beasts

At the moment when the blade and stone destroyed the clay of Abel Did the thirst of Lilith grow, like serpents slithering from her cunt And danced upon my spine, burning tendons as Satan stood watching

LOOK INTO MIRROR AND VISUALIZE SELF

A dragon woke in my flesh, the slug-slimed saliva of the dead flesh of Abel was ignited in the Blackened Lightening of a Serpent, and did then this fire arise up to me.

In this moment of death did life emerge, a wolf whose pulsating member violated with welcomed abandon the whore who sought the flesh of Lilith, turned gaping and dripping jaw up towards the burning sun, which was eclipsed by the Moon, and a serpent hissed towards the moon with fangs and tongue knowing the depths of the womb of my own Spiritual mother, Lilith unto me at the moment of orgasm and death!

Cain as I am now as a God, yet cursed by the sheep fucking majority, their farming communities denouncing those who seek a isolation beyond their understanding. Satan be thy name, as my father the Devil!

PUT DAGGER DOWN & HOLD CHALICE UP

The fruits of the Skull had opened up, drinking deep of the blood and venom of the Cup from a spirit-less skull, did I devour and seek the Beast within! My Demon was now fed, feasting with the heat and lust as the torn core of a woman, whose serpent tongue flickered me to spilling seed in her teeth ripping womb.

I drink the blood of my father in the honor
of the Sun and the Moon!"

DRINK FROM CHALICE

COENA DOMINI SATHANAS
PART II
The Flesh HOLD UP PLATE OF MEAT:

Behold, the flesh is the nourishment of the shadows, let us eat this flesh in remembrance of the first falling stone and blade, let us praise the darkness which lifted Cain up as the Son of the Beast!

The Blood:

(Holding the Skull cup or chalice) – *Let us drink in honor of the first blood split, that first hungering gleam of the wolf on its prey, the first taste of the elixir of life which nourished the skin of the Great Whore, that very desire which deflowers the Holy Virgin, who became as our whore. Let us drink in honor of Samael the Father and Cain the Son. With this blood do our eyes open!*

The Sacrifice:

(Ceremonial) – Destroy images you are familiar with in your life which are concerning a form of stagnation and repression

– religious or other. Create an ambience of blasphemy and self-liberation.

PRACTICING MAGICK CONSISTENTLY

Magick is the act of causing change both within and then outside of the self. Magick, like Yoga or any other act improves with practice. As you begin a process of initiation keep in mind that it is not a part-time Religion like Christianity or a hobby. Magick is a part of your life, living and breathing. Your Spirit – Mind – Body are equally affected, driven and supported by Magick. When you are at your lowest, when you feel alone, there is Magick. When you are at the top of the world, there is Magick. Be prepared to listen to your instincts, drive yourself beyond your limits.

Magick should be made a daily practice – set aside time each day to practice your process of meditation – controlling the mind, slowing your thoughts, etc. You can find suitable practice in THE BIBLE OF THE ADVERSARY.

You will want to begin with exercises which control the body and mind, for instance Ahrimanic Yoga. It is essential to set aside practice daily for magickal work. Nothing will prove detrimental to your development than falling off from practice. You must be prepared to strengthen yourself through discipline. This very discipline will support your magickal development later on.

You must be prepared to hold yourself to your goals. For everything you do, there must be a measurable involved. If you wish to overcome a smoking habit: have your meditation techniques shown progress? If not, prepare to change them quickly. If you wish to get in shape, you invocations to Aeshma the Daeva of aggression should charge you – if not, ask yourself why? If it is discipline, focus on steps daily and you will affect discipline.

1. Know your goal which affects your physical life foremost.

-I wish to get in shape and improve the energy level within a period of two months.

2. Know the initiatory goal of what will affect your initiatory process.

- By getting in shape I can perform yoga in a more proficient way. This will result in a more meaningful process to align my mind in a meditative state.

Measurable progress:

-After the first few times of exercise, establish a harrowing goal to achieve in the 2 months. This may involve weight lifting, running, sit ups or any similar activity.

Keep a journal on your activity.

Learn a Yatukih nirang from THE BIBLE OF THE ADVERSARY. Perform Staota or mantra while conducting exercise.

ALTAR & TOOLS

The ritual tools within the Luciferian Tradition are as various as the witches themselves. Some create fetish servitors, embodied and often created demonic familiars bound to objects, created from animal remains, blood or sexual fluids to form a visualized shade which holds significance to the sorcerer himself. Some create dolls and others use little or no exterior tools or implements. What holds tradition among such Adepts is the commitment of the Luciferic Spirit within. This is the mind of the practitioner which has been liberated through antinomian practices and thought, by this determined focus that the Will of the Black Adept has transformed he or she into a Daemonic Being. Within ancient Persian practice, the Ahriman (Satan) created daemon Akoman (meaning Evil Mind) is the Luciferian Mind which seeks liberation and independence from the mass or herd mentality, to become something 'other' by the forbidden or 'evil' path of Magick or Witchcraft.

Certain tools within the Craft Sinister are often considered 'haunted' objects, empowered by ongoing ritual practice by the witch or sorcerer which gives the fetish a seeming life independent from their own, however always usually in accordance to their Will. Ritual instruments such as the Tibetan Kangling, a Trumpet made from the thigh bone of a hanged man, a ritual knife known as an Athame, according to Idries Shah as 'adhdhame' being 'bloodletter', used in Sabbat ritual practice to focus the Will or Cast the Mind into the determined direction of ritual Magick; the blade representing the Luciferic Mind of the magician. The Skull Cup, made from the top part of the human skull, makes a drinking bowl used in ceremonial or solitary practice. None of these ritual tools are required for practice, which depends solely on the means and predilection of the sorcerer.

ALTAR

The altar is the area of working in which the sorcerer projects their will upon the universe. The altar should be adorned in implements which signify the desire and aim of the Luciferian. If unable to have a real altar, for instance if you are in the military, or living somewhere in which an altar would prove a negative addition, then create your ideal altar via the imagination. This can provide a powerful tool in your magickal work as this is the foundation of the path – the mind. The altar and the inverted pentagram often represent the Mastery of the Earth. Thus the Altar belongs to the essence of Belial, fixed earth, foundation.

CHALICE

The cup represents the aspects of the subconscious brought into flesh, Leviathan rising from the abyss. The sorcerer drinks from a chalice often at the end of a rite to symbolize confirmation of the ritual itself, the intent to make flesh. Some magickians use skull caps to drink from, representing the power of the carnal and the spiritual plane.

CANDLES – COLOR AND MEANING

Color appeals to sight, allowing such to assist in inspiring your ceremonial rituals is paramount. When preparing for a specific ritual, think of the colors you will use in your rites. The main candles used in Luciferian rites is BLACK and RED, but there are so many other colors to consider for rituals. In working with the Watchers/Grigori, the Luciferian will use yellow, blue, white and green among others. Don't limit yourself in color for corresponding rituals. Here are a few descriptions and suggestions.

Black : Hidden Knowledge, Death, Power, Change and Defense

Red: Creativity, Love, Desire, Attraction, Vitality, War and Aggression

White: Self-Deification (think SUN card of the LUCIFERIAN TAROT) Purity, Cleansing, Protection and Bestowing Health to Another

Blue: Happiness, Work (Obtaining Job, Change of Career) and Friendship

Yellow: Health, Happiness, Wits and Alertness = Intuition,
Green: Money, Success and Material Items
Orange: Endurance, thought, and inspiration.
Purple: Sex and Rejuvenation.

SIGIL OF INFERNAL UNION

NORTH - BELIAL - EARTH - PENTACLE
STABILITY - PHYSICAL WELL BEING, POWER

**WEST -
LEVIATHAN
WATER
CUPS**
Emotion,
subconscious
dreams

**EAST -
LUCIFER
AIR -
SWORDS**
intelligence
wisdom,
self-illumination

SOUTH - SATAN - FIRE - WAND
COURAGE, PASSION SPIRIT

These are the Luciferian meanings of the Sigil of Infernal Union. As you can see, there is no negativity. The Luciferian spirit is about conquering; hell is as meaningful as heaven. Think of these attributes in your workings and every day life.

THE INVERTED PENTAGRAM

The pentagram is traditionally a symbol of summoning spirits, the elements which create human consciousness are represented as the upright pentagram. The inverted pentagram is a symbol of the "Fire" of Lucifer brought to man. It also represents the power of the Goat or Lust, Azazel and that which is balanced with Spirit.

It is important to understand what the Inverted Pentagram actually means, the small, often overlooked details have deep meaning which will present interesting perspectives for those willing to explore them. As you can see with Lucifer, the

"Prince of the Powers of the Air" represents the bringer of wisdom and intelligence.

ALGOL

The Sigil of ALGOL (above) is a symbol of power with the origin of self. The Chaos Star represents disorder and rebellion, the force which begets change. The inverted pentagram represents the essence of Ahriman or Samael, the Adversarial spirit along with his equal Lilith or Az-Jeh, the Fiery Goddess with creates balance. The Algol sigil is dual, it is chaos but DIRECTED, or Willed into existence. Algol as named from the constellation is the "Head of Satan" or the Willed Adversarial power. Many Luciferians use this symbol in Magick and self-transformation. The Algol Sigil does not represent "evil" or "destruction" in any moralistic or behaviorial anti-social associations. More on ALGOL may be found in LIBER HVHI- Magick of the Adversary.

THE BLADE OR ATHAME

THE ATHAME OR BLADE OF THE WHITE HILT

The Athame is the blood letter or Blade of Luciferian Magick. It is different from the Black Hilted Knife as it relates to works of Self-illumination, of Transformative Magick. You may purchase a blade and consecrate it. Consecrating the blade is through a ritual it will be cleansed and prepared for use just by yourself and no one else. The Blade should be made in the hour of Mercury when in the sign of the Ram or Scorpion. You may alternatively conduct such when the Moon is Waning in a more probable time frame.

Practice well in the light of Diabolus. Cain is also traditionally viewed as the Witch Father who blessed the Athame or Ritual Knife by the metal from a fallen meteor, or Lucifer's Forge and flame consecrates the blade of sorcery.

CONSECRATION

Consecration is the act of preparing ritual tools for their use in Magick. As Magick is a sacred art, your tools will be sacred as well.

STEPS FOR CONSECRATING THE ATHAME-

1. When the Moon is waning, fill a bucket or basin with distilled and purified water and pour salt, Abramelin Oil and a few drops of your own blood.

2. You will then wish to have a small fire which you will hold the blade over. As it is heated in the flame, envision the fires of Azazel and Hecate, purifying and blessing the blade with your divine Will. It is the very blade which once consecrated, should be seen as forged by Cain from the metal from Lucifer's Crown, in the very Forge of Cain does the Fire of Iblis bless.

3. When the blade is heated, take the knife and place it in the water –

By the Blood I give I empower this Blade, the very knife of my Divine Will

By the Moon Waxing and Waning I do receive the Fallen Stars fiery and ancient

Blade of steel do I summon thee, with the fires of Azazel called Shaitan do I consecrate thee, by the flames of Hecate do I empower thee!

The circle is cast in the Sabbat journey of the Celestial and Infernal –

Blessed is this sacred blade –From the meteor which fell from the crown of Lucifer!

By the metal blessed in the fiery forge of Our Lord Daeva, who is Cain the Cloaked One So mote it be!

THE BLACK HILTED KNIFE (Evocation Dagger)

The Black Hilted Knife is the blade of Barbarous Evocation, the knife dedicated to Shaitan of Midnight and Banal, the Daemonic Adversarial Blade of Lucifer, the sacred weapon of banishing and commanding – the fulgaris lightning bolt of the fallen Djinn.

The Black Hilted Knife is used for making the circle and commanding the spirits into the Triangle, the sacred circle within the meeting place of spirits. You would use this dagger when performing rites of sorcery and goetic magick.

STEPS FOR CONSECRATING THE EVOCATION DAGGER

1. The Blade may be consecrated in the hour of Saturn. As well when the moon is waning create a distilled water container and fill with blackened pepper, Hecate Oil and a few drops of your own blood. With the flame burning, hold the blade within allowing it to be consumed.
2. While holding the blade in the flames, envision the fires of the underworld, of Hecate-Lilith and Banal, of the Daemonic Gods below who open the gates of our own transformation. Envision the fire empowering the blade with the serpent tongue of Shaitan of Midnight, the purifier of the black handled knife.
3. As the blade is immersed in the water, recite-

By the Mysteries of the Depths, the Coiling Dragon of Old
Beheld to the Gates of Leviathan
By Hecate and the Skull Wreathed in Roses, which is silence and beauty
I summon thee blade of steel, envenomed in the Darkness of the Earth
Do become knife of the Devil's Claw, my sacred tool of summoning
Water-Daemon of the Blade be born
By Banal and those of the shadowed realms-
Blade be blessed! So mote it be!!

RITUAL CONSTRUCTION

All rituals should have structure and intent for performing. When you enter the ritual chamber, you are opening doors to your subconscious or beyond. The sense of Discipline, Will and focus is paramount to the success of the ritual.

Let's explore the definitions of the types of ritual.

EVOCATION

Evocation is the art of summoning and controlling spirits for a specific purpose, within a ritual setting. Evocation often includes subconscious automata, spirits, created wraith-forms and so on. In the Luciferian methodology, magickians evoke spirit or deific masks (powers given anthropomorphic attributes). Evocations fall under the category of Sorcery as often such is meant for commanding and controlling a force for a specific purpose based in life. It may be spiritual defence, to obtain a lover, good luck, to achieve something, etc.

SIGILS AND SYMBOLS

"Sigils are monograms of thought, for the government of energy"

"Sigils are the art of believing, my invention for making belief organic, ergo, true belief."- Austin Spare, The Book of Pleasure.

Within Magick, Sigils or Talismans are based on the foundation of Will and Imagination, both of which are the very fuel points for which Sigils may work. Sigils were used widely in ceremonial magick, elder grimoires which give specific symbols representing spirits. A suitable magickian is able to create his or hers, even using an already created sigil to empower and utilize in ritual. Here we will focus on charging a pre-made sigil.

The method for charging spirits relates to the self. Here is a brief model:

SELF + Will – Imagination (activation point, Imagination is everything.) + Spirit.

Sigils are the language of the subconscious. It has been mistakenly thought that sigils are letter combinations in the style of Austin Osman Spare. This is not correct by any means. Just as magick is personal to the individual, and each sorcerer has his or her own personal system, so it is with the methods of sigil magick. The conscious mind must forget what the significance of the sigil is in order for the subconscious to absorb it and set it's fleshing in motion.

The Sigil of Lucifer

The Sigil of Lucifer, for instance, is used by many Luciferians who wish to call forth the Spirit intelligence in the "Azal'ucel" rite, which is essentially the Holy Guardian Angel or the higher self. We will try here a different method of utilizing the Lucifer Sigil, perhaps making it more "simple", then using it in a ritual setting.

CONSTRUCTION OF SIGILS

While we will not employ the details of the methods of Austin Osman Spare, we will utilize some of the foundations of his concepts – SIMPLICITY.

As see with the Lucifer sigil, it contains four characters – one circle and three separate shapes. When beginning in Magick, the focus and concentration points are critical in ritual, thus the image must be simple until the magickian masters the basics. Let's take the elements which stand out the most in the Lucifer sigil and combind them to a perhaps more simplistic sigil:

The sigil is now contained within a circle, completing a focus for the magickian to visualize the main points of the talisman.

You may copy, draw or print this sigil on a parchment, or wood, anything which is suitable for you. It should be small enough to carry with you – perhaps a parchment paper with a leather backing.

Charging the sigil – you would utilize the evocation method employed in the Yatukih Sorcery section of THE BIBLE OF THE ADVERSARY, or in the "RITUAL OF AZAL'UCEL". Goetic Sorcery is of course equally potent when applied with Will and Imagination.

Here are some basic steps:

1. Construct Sigil – sigil must reflect a specific desire you wish to achieve i.e. new job, insight into subconscious, hidden wisdom (Luciferian Angel or Azal'ucel), etc.

2. Perform a ritual to evoke the spirit and bind it to Sigil – numerous methods in THE BIBLE OF THE

ADVERSARY are employed. We will use the Luciferian Goetia method in this book.

3. Constrain the spirit via techniques above.
4. Close ritual. The sigil will be charged. Once you have charged the sigil it becomes a talisman – carry it on you, when you see it, visualize the outcome you wish.

INVOCATION

Invocation is the art of calling spirits within, which are called often "Deific Masks" or anthropomorphic associations of energy. No matter if you are an Atheist or a Theistic Luciferian, invocation brings results. You may approach it as an aspect of your consciousness, with invocation brining this subconscious knowledge to the forefront, you may view it as possession, a spirit inhabiting your psyche during invocation, to impart wisdom by the act, you may approach it as a Spirit entering you via your subconscious, both powers brought together to raise up in the magickians' consciousness. Invocation essentially is the art in which the Magickian adopts the identity of the Deific Mask or God form.

DEFINITIONS / OBJECTIVES

Here we will briefly explore the definitions and objectives of rituals, why certain things are done and the goals of such workings.

Action	Meaning
Cast Circle	Clear mind/focus
Statement of intent	Goal of working
Invocation	Calling spirits within
Close circle	Clearing mind
Banish	Clear area

STATEMENT OF INTENT

A statement of intent is significant as it represents the intent of the magickian performing the ritual. It keeps the conscious mind focused in the beginning of the process – it allows the seed the begin to form in the subconscious as well. Often, a suitable statement begins with "It is my will....".

FOCUS ON SIGIL/INVOCATION/EVOCATION

During invocation your Will should be focused on the sigil and visualizing the spirit you are calling forth. It is always significant to set your ritual to visually, sonically or otherwise embody the spirit you are calling forth. Sounds, music, imagry, all of these things support invocation.

CHARGING A SIGIL

During the ritual, charging the ritual is important. Some magickians will cut themselves and put a small amount of blood on the sigil – this gives material basis – foundation and a symbolic "life" offering to the spirit being called. Some use sexual fluids to charge sigils or even animal skin, nails or otherwise based on the spirit. In the Yatukih Sorcery path, skin, ashes and bones are considered powerful enough to create daevas or demons.

BANISH

Banishing is the process of closing the ritual and clearing the mind. In Luciferian Rites, the magickian does not banish spirits – he or she clears their own circle of being, allows the mind to forget the work so it may take charge in the subconscious mind.

CHANTING

The use of chanting in magick and ritual is a powerful tool which stimulates and focuses the mind. Chanting has been used since Magick has first emerged, thousands of years ago. Mantras are forms of words combinded together which initially have meaning but when constructed phoenetically loose conscious meaning. The subconscious mind, however remembers the meaning and when recited stimulates and acts as a "invocation" of the force of which the word derives. Rhythmic and sequential use of the Mantra is significant as the vibrations ring out and charge the ritual with the necessary ambience. This is why prayers no matter in what religion can bring results – this belief is fundamental to success in ritual magick. In THE BIBLE OF THE ADVERSARY, you will find STAOTAS as a major part of Yatukih Sorcery. Staotas are vibrations of sound which effect the ritual in a major way.

DREAMING

The expression of the subconscious is often first displayed via dreams. Dreaming is a natural process of living and the mind exploring different concepts and considerations. Austin Osman Spare considered dreaming to be a major factor in his system of sorcery. It is suggested that you keep a dream journal, this is different from a magickal journal as you are just documenting dreams and the first impressions upon waking. Keep in mind many elements are forgotten fifteen minutes after waking, if you could write down a few lines every time you have a dream think of the details you will save. This of course takes discipline to do everytime, even a bit of planning. If you set your alarm to wake 30 minutes before you are due to work or an appointment, you won't be able or have the discipline to write it down. Plan and relax.
Remember to mark well your nightmares, these are perhaps the most important experiences in your sleeping cycle that you may have. The God Set is also the God of Nightmares, embrace them. Dreaming is very significant in astral projection, being a significant point to Vampyric Magick.

SCRYING

Scrying has long been the art of the gifted witch or magickian who is able to enter a trance like state and receive visions. Scrying has been an art used by shamans since recorded history. There are numerous methods of scrying, tools such as black mirrors, considered by the ancient Hebrews as the gateway to the caves of Lilith, tea leaves, geomantic vibration, reading auras to ancient times such as reading entrails. Those who use black mirrors may concentrate on this with little light in their ritual area; many things may "come across" to them.

INVOCATION

The following ritual is a powerful foundational invocation rite, of calling Samael and Lilith within. Upon growing adept at this invocation, the next process of invocation is the "RITUAL OF AZAL'UCEL" as found in THE BIBLE OF THE ADVERSARY.

THE RITUAL OF INFERNAL UNION

This is a Solitary ritual based on the union of opposites.

You will want to have a Black Robe

Two Candles: Black and Red, Chalice and Athame

The altar piece should be the infernal union sigil above the altar or upon it.

The Grand Luciferian Circle is what you will stand within; the point should face the north.

You will need to create a statement of intent; you may write it down or memorize it.

A statement of intent would read as the following:

"It is my Will to invoke the Egregores of Samael and Lilith, so that by union of Both within myself, I shall become reborn as Baphomet."

Perform banishing ritual[5] to clear mind and Call the Four Quarters:

Recite facing altar, vibrate 9 times:

Zazas, Zazas, Nasatanada Zazas

(Visualize the Mouth of Hell opening forth)

FACING THE SOUTH:

Samael,

Lords of the Southern Tower, Djinn Father of fire and desert sands, I do summon thee forth to witness my rites of awakening and union. I command the fires of the Abyss to protect my circle, let the gates be opened!

EAST:

Lucifer-Phosphorus,

Lords of the Eastern Tower, bearer of the black flame, lord of light and Promethean flame, I do summon thee forth to witness my rites of awakening and union. I command the forces of Air and the astral plane send thy Luciferian elementals to guard this circle.

WEST:

Leviathan-Ourabouris,

Lord of the Western Tower, who beholds the Black Flame hidden in the depths!

---

[5] Casting the circle of Cain or one from THE BIBLE OF THE ADVERSARY.

Great encircling one, who holds the keys to immortality! I summon the forces of Water and the Sea to witness my rites of awakening and union. Be watchful and protect this circle!

NORTH:

Belial,

Lord of the Northern Tower, who fell from heaven to be as God itself, who accepts no master- I do summon thee forth to witness my rites of awakening and union. I command the forces of the earth to protect this circle!

Imagine each force in a silent way adding the essence of protection around you.

TAKE NOW THE ATHAME FROM THE ALTAR, ENVISION THE IMAGE OF SAMAEL, RECITING:

"Solar force of fire and inspiration, which from all life emerges as its own being; I do summon thee, Samael from the depths of my soul, my very being, to emerge in my consciousness as life and solar force! Do manifest and hear my words, which are meant as an invocation of Sorath, the Beast 666 which is your secret name. Samael, Satan do manifest unto me. Let me guide the union of opposites!"

Allow the force to become intertwined with your consciousness; share the ecstasy with this angel of fire and light.

TAKE NOW THE CUP FROM THE ALTAR, DRINKING DEEPLY OF ITS COLD AND REFRESHING ELIXIR.

Envision now Lilith and recite:

"Lunar force of water and dream walking, which you shall manifest my consciousness from the desert caves of the Red Sea, I do summon you, invoke you within me. Bring unto me your mysteries of your children, the Lilitu, that I may hold the arcana of sexual union and vampiric manifestation. Enter me, mother of the path of the wise; reveal your bestial and angelic essence to me. Do manifest through me now, join in union with your mate, Samael. Join through me the union of Opposites!"

Allow the lunar energy to flow through you, catching the visions of lilitu and such succubi, bestial and hair covered below their waste...seeking the sexual union of others in great fornication and abandonment. Lilith is Babalon, the goddess who bathes in the blood of the moon.

FACE NOW THE ALTAR, TAKE THE WAND AND RECITE WHILE FOCUSING UPON LILITH:

"She howls upon the desert winds, as the moon brings the cloak of Darkness. The shadows radiate her essence, blood drinker, devouress of the sleeping, fornicate in the spilt veins of those who come to you!

Lilith, LA-KAL-IL-LI-KA, I invoke thee by your sacred names:

Abeko, Batna, Abito, Eilo, Amizo, Ita, Izorpo, Kali, Kea, Kokos, Odam, Patrota, Podo, Partasah, Satrina, Talto, Lilith!

And by your other names of calling:

Abyzu, Ailo, Alu, Abro, Amiz, Amizu, Ardad lili, Avitu, Bituah, Gelou, Gallu, Gilou, Ik, Kalee, Ils, Kakash, Lamassu, Kema, Partashah, Petrota, Pods, Raphi, Satrinah, Thiltho, Zahriel, Zefonith, Lilith!

By the words of Power:

BABALON-BAL-BIN-ABRAFT, ASAL-ON-AI, ATHOR-E-BAL-O, ERESHKIGAL!

I offer my essence as sacrifice, a drop of my blood. Witch Queen of the infernal Sabbat! I do invoke thee, horned moon which spills and drinks the lunar blood, she who fornicates with Daemons, I do seek your kiss, I give you substance now from which you shall enter me!

Lilith, beautiful mother, giver of life and desire, I do summon thee forth! Lilith, who resides in the caves with your children of darkness, spawned through once congress with Samael, I unite now your passion through creation!"

Face now the Altar, envision the Red Dragon who changes into the form of the fallen Seraphim, Samael, and recite:

"Whom fell from heavenly unlight to have knowledge of the darkness, fallen seraph of fire and the sun, I do invoke thee, Samael. To you, who has walked the earth for thousands of years, from body to body, now shall you spread your light unto humanity.

Angel, known as Shemna'il, who is Nasiru'd-Din, I do invoke thee, solar force, known as Sorath, Beast whose number is of the Sun itself, I do summon thee forth! Serpent Angel, who came by the astral plane with Melek Taaus, known as

Shaitan, Lucifer – the Brothers of Light. Come forth now through me, manifest in my being, we shall join as one. By the names of power:

AR-O-GO-GO-RU-ABRAO, PUR, IAFTH, OO, AR, THIAF, A-THELE-BER-SET, PHITHETA-SOE!!

I summon thee, revealed as Set, whom is the sun and darkness in union!"

Envison now the fire of spirit, which is swirling within your very self, encircling Lilith and moving throughout your consciousness.

TAKE NOW THE ATHAME AND FOCUS UPON THE DRAGON-ANGEL, LEVIATHAN.

"Force of the Subconscious, whom I call the outside, I do summon thee to bring The Sun and the Moon, Samael and Lilith, in glorious union! I do Will this union within my self, that I may speak the words unheard from the profane, and my Will manifest through the gates of Apep!

Hear the word of power:

MRIODOM!!

Allow now the self to experience grand ecstasy, that through enflaming the self one would focus upon the image of Samael and Lilith in sexual congress, the fire and water of spirit joining in a blaze of force.

"Ya! Zat-I Shaitan! <u>So it is done.</u>

INVOCATION TO AZ
The Great Demon Whore –
Mother of Witchcraft

AZ first appeared as a weapon given to Ahriman. It was said Ahriman gave an attack on the spiritual world[6], and he was thrown back into the Abyss for a time. Many demons sought to raise Ahriman from his great sleep and nothing would work. The Great Whore came forth to awaken Ahriman, and woke him with stating that she would "Take away the dignity of Blessed Man". Ahriman stood and glowed with unnatural life and came from the Abyss again. This "Demon Whore"[7] as referred is none other than AZ, the "weapon of concupiscence." AZ[8] is the Witch Queen and Bride of Ahriman, a Mother of Demons. The flesh she takes later is that of Lilith, the Hebrew Demon Queen who was the embodiment of sorcery, succubi and sexual congress. AZ represents that which is most feared among all religions, Women as a Strong and cunning force. It is also written that the Devil's (Ahriman) Kiss causes menstruation, and such is a highly abhorred occurrence among the Zoroastrians.

Az is also closely connected in Buddhism, and is an enemy of the Buddhist mind. The principle of the cause of conditioned existence is a word, *Avidya*, meaning 'ignorance' and such a principle manifestation is *trshna*, being 'Thirst'. AZ devours and drinks deep the lifeblood in a desire for continued existence in time. She is isolate and individual consciousness, a dual Bearer of the Black Flame. She is matched only by Ahriman, the Prince of Darkness.

---

[6] The Teachings of the Magi, R.C. Zaehner, London 1956

[7] Selections of Zatsparam and The Dawn and Twilight of the Zoroastrianism, R.C. Zachner, NY 1961

[8] AZ is concupiscence, lust and greed – she is also called Varan, which is sexual desire and interestingly enough Religious Doubt. This is symbolic of the rebellious and Luciferian Mind, that which perceives itself and doubts higher authority. Az is this force which take in anthropomorphic form, LILITH, and the Witch Woman who frees herself from bonds. Az is also a balancing force within Man, and Ahriman and Az awakened is a comparable magickal formula to Aleister Crowley's Beast and Babalon Conjoined.

The People of the Lie, those who are initiated by spiritual deed in the Yatuk Dinoih are Left Hand Path practitioners, that is, we seek to isolate, strengthen and promote continued existence beyond the traps of flesh, but through flesh as well. We, just as Ahriman, love life, and seek to make it stronger by means of self-deification through antinomian thought. When approaching AZ as the Queen of the Circle, know that she too resides with the Dead, yet she does not devour them always. AZ may also be considered the same as the Hindu KALI (interestingly enough, one of the 17 names of LILITH) and Hecate, the Grecian Goddess of the Dead.

TEMPLE:

1. To be adorned in images of death, crimson and the feminine aspects of dark witchcraft, such as Babalon riding the Dragon, Kali, Lilith, Hel and all of the dark goddesses of Wicca, Luciferian Witchcraft and other mythologies throughout history.
2. The altar itself should be adorned in crimson and shades of blood red, with the sigil of Babalon hanging in the front of the altar. Keep in mind this force is the universal Daemonic Goddess, she takes many forms all of which are difficult for the uninitiated to understand. Keep this ritual to yourself if you or anyone in your coven performs it. This rite is designed to issue forth the Dragon goddess to manifest in either the Witch or the Warlock, regardless of sexual preference, gender orientation and identification. Each individual within the path of the Yatuk Dinoih should be prepared to explore both the feminine aspects of their being as well as the masculine. Unity is through moving through opposites.
3. A chalice filled with elixir of your choice.
4. The Black Hilted Knife or Evocation Dagger.
5. Light red and black candles; both aspects of Az-Babalon.

Above: The Sigil of Babalon – Az · Lilith

As you perform the ritual of Az, visualize clearly the woman of your dreams – this could be what you want most in a mate, if you are a woman the aspects of which you seek to become will grow clearer. As you invoke, visualize your self as Babalon or this force speaking through you.

"The Abyss which gave me being has no bounds over my existence. I, who am known as the Blood Goddess AZ stands before the Eye of Ahriman, awakened and alive. I hold the cup of fornication, the elixir of life, to announce and rejoice in my divinity. I am the Great Whore, presiding over the Sabbat of witches, to let all taste of my joys. I stand before all other white goddesses, those who in their happy fields have grown from my darkness, my shadow to proclaim them as unfertile, barren and rotting from their fear and lack of balance. I kiss them gently as a mother then with a movement of my mind, rape and spill their blood into my cup of desire. I am the goddess of death and life. I join in rapture with the Infernal Dragon, Samael · Ahriman, whom brings my joy in rapture and union.

Upon the back of the Beast I ride, and brought forth the Antichrist who shall grow unseen before and through many. The age of ignorance and servitude is over. The While fornicating, call my names that are many, AZ, BABALON, LILITH. Spill your seed in my name, in my glory and in my desire. I am the model for which all women shall seek to channel. My gateway is through ecstasy, through the mirror, between the breasts of the scarlet woman.

I stand before the impotent mother called Mary and laugh at her sterile incompetence. This failure of a mother and feeble spirit that cowers behind her son is to be no more! For every woman who cannels and invokes me, whom shall take the name of Witch and Scarlet Woman shall one by erase her manifestation in this world. I shall bring the doctrines of Witchcraft through a new method, which shall be of twilight workings many can embrace. I shall not reveal all of which I am to them, as they cannot grasp my terror and beauty. This need not concern them, as my Will shall manifest through each Goddess who dares invoke me! I spit in the mouth of impotence and within me shall you find the Union of Opposition.

HOLD THE CUP UP TO THE SIGIL OF BABALON

I am within all and may be summoned by the vessel of the skull....the blood is the life!

I am Vampyre, I am shadow, I am the Devouring Demon which drains the life of the weak, I give the Blackened Flame of Life to those who may face me...

Azi...Azaka...Babalon....Nasu...AZ..AZ....AZ!

EVOCATION
LUCIFERIAN GOETIA METHOD

THE CONJURATIONS

The Luciferian Goetia method does not employ Christian conjurations, as does the traditional Lemegethon. To use Christian conjurations in a Luciferian ideology is pointless and self-degrading.

We will use the Sigil of Paimon for example.

The 72 Spirits of the Shemhamforasch

Utilizing a basic method of circle conjurations, place the sigil of Paimon within the center of the Triangle of Evocation. You may hold your evocation dagger pointed to the circle of Paimon, the dagger is the symbolic act of affirming Will and commanding change accordingly. Recite the invocations with passion, filling your spirit and mind with inspiration and living with each word.

"I do summon and evoke thee, O' Spirit N. by the Flames of Azazel – the Lord of the Earth I conjure thee forth. By Beralanensis, Baldachiensis, Paumachia and Aplogiae Sedes; by the most powerful Guardians, Djinn, Genii and the Spirits of the Abyss, brought forth by the Great Shadow of the Fire Seraph. I summon thee wise and ancient spirits, attend me and appear now in this circle-

By the names of Lucifer, who brought the Flame unto the Clay – He that gave us breath, Immortal and Holy Fire.

Lucifer, Ouyar, Chameron, Aliseon, Mandousin, Premy, Oriet, Naydru, Esmay, Eparinesont, Estiot, Dumosson, Panochar, Casmiel, Hayras, Fabelleronthou, Sadirno, Peatham, Venite, Venite, Lucifer Amen.

I summon thee, shadow and light, Angel and Daemon, together as one...I do summon these O great familiar of the earth, from which my Dagger commands thee, appear and move, materialize in this meeting place of spirits. I conjure thee, Spirit N. who shall appear before me, in circle and center. Attend now my calling and show thyself in a form you so desire that we may hold congress in the communion of my self!"

OPTIONAL ENGLISH/ENOCHIAN CONJURATION-

Some magickians find Enochian to be a compelling tongue for rituals.

"I do conjure thee, O' spirit N. by the flames of Azazel – the Lord of the Earth I conjure thee forth. By Beralanensis, Baldachiensis, Paumachia and Aplogiae Sedes; by the most powerful Guardians and spirits of the Beast, brought forth by the mighty throne, I summon thee descending spirits, dragon of the dark heavens

By the crown of the Dragon, enthroned Eye of Holy Fire – Be friendly unto me, enter this circle and bring forth your wisdom and truth, descend and come forth from the Dragon's Temple, bring forth the Wisdom of the Wicked."

(Translated)-

OL GNAY ZODANETA GAH IALPRG AZAZEL, ENAY THAHAAOTAHE OL ZODAMETA – MICMA – MICMA MICALZ BRANSG GAH A ORH LEVITHMONG YOLCAM OXIAYAL IALPOR GAH – OL VINU ARPHE GAH, VOVIM DE A MAHORELA IALPRT MOMAO DE A VOVIM, VEL UCORSAPAX OOANOAN DE PIRE IALPRT ZORSE PAMBT OL, ZIMII OI COMSELH VOLCAM G ANANAEL VOOAN UNIGLAG NIISA VOVIM SIAION YOLCAM ANANAEL DE BABALON.

THE INVOCATION OF THE KING

Being Amaimon, Gaap, Paimon or Asmoday

Upon performing the initial evocation, you will wish to invoke the higher spirits who have compelling power, thus focusing and summoning forth the following will provide a certain power-focus to encircle the spirits you seek.

"Great – Powerful King Amaimon, who exalted in the Power of the Spirits in the Kingdom of the East, (South, West or North) I invoke thee in the name of Darkness, from the dwelling of darkness and in their power of illumination. In the name of Primeumaton who reigns over the palaces of the Sun and the Moon – I invoke thee to appear before this circle, in this triangle – the very gathering place of spirits. I seek Amaimon to Rise up in me as MAHAZAEL, the devouring dragon. Open thy eyes through mine Amaimon and I shall have thy Blackened Flame within.

Great King Gaap, bring to me the knowledge of the Black Flame, rise up in me and open my eyes to the world and the power within it.

Great Spirit Paimon, Luciferic Angel, awaken within me and bring the wisdom of ages.

Asmoday, Give unto me the power of the 7, that I may be as the Beast upon the Earth. Arise through me as I become the One adorned in fire.

Thou art fallen and perfected Angel, who hath tasted the ecstasies As above and So below, Sun nourished Djinn who drank deep of the shadows, whose sword tortures those who would obey me not ·. I call and Command o' king N. to bring this spirit unto me without violence or harm – This is my Will. "

THE CONSTRAINT

Constraining the spirit is necessary in affirming the energy you are focusing into the evocation triangle.

"I do conjure and summon thee, Spirit N. by the flaming essence of the Forked Stave of the Sun, the Adversarial Shadow and Burning Fire which is the Prince of Spirits, Angels and Daemon. Come thou forth and without delay to me, Spirit N. By Adonai, the Lord of the Earth, By the Axis of the Sun and the Moon I summon thee. By the Eternal Fire, come now unto this Circle...Be welcomed unto me."

WELCOME UNTO THE SPIRIT

"Welcome Spirit N. You are welcomed in this meeting place within the Crossroads. I have summoned you forth, to join with me, by the union of Heaven and Hell. I bind this within this circle, take flesh and desire within thy Sigil of Calling, which I shall give unto thee life. Thou shalt not leave this circle until I am satisfied, for I shall bring you forth into the world of flesh once again.

By the sacred center of the Arcanum of Shadow and Light, within the Ourabouris Circle I am bound and free, yet as you are Spirit N. shall you enflesh my desires of which I speak. By my command and Will do you bring forth that which I have called you for, that I shall also seek your servitors, those whom obey your command.

By the Pentacle of Solomon have I summoned thee! Give unto me a True Answer"

LICENCE TO DEPART

"Hail to thee Spirit N., thou hast answered my questions, and has caused no harm or danger to man or beast. You may depart now unto your place of rest and repose. Be with me in dreams and in flesh as I desire, yet thou art free to leave this dwelling at Will. This sigil will be your gateway, allow your spirits to dwell within it. So it is done. One may command the spirit in the vessel within the triangle, just as one would summon the spirit into visible appearance."

SORCERY

Sorcery is the art of encircling, or visualizing strongly, your desire. Sorcery is from the ancient Sumerian word meaning "to encircle" and is considered a method first taught by the Grigori or Watchers. Sorcery is called a form of Magick which is "low" as it relates to basic desires. Within the Luciferian Witchcraft path, there are considered three avenues of Magick: Luciferian Magick – Developing the self, Therionick Sorcery – Lycanthropy and Bestial Sorcery and Yatukih Sorcery – Daemonic Magick and Sorcery based in ancient Avestan spirits. We will not go too deeply into the three aspects, but general Sorcery and Magick here within the Yatukih path. Let's first get familiar with the foundations and basics of summoning spirits.

When you cast spells or evoke powers, you should always make sure there is a "buy in" from yourself. You must find associations or inspirations to charge you; it should be inspiring to perform this type of magick! If you utilize an image in your sorcery to obtain results; do it. The point of sorcery is to achieve results.

AHRIMAN

Ahriman or Angra Mainyu is the ancient Persian spirit or demon of darkness. A God associated with the Yatuk Dinoih[9], the ancient Persian system of hidden witchcraft and sorcery. Ahriman was the shadow which existed between the veils of light and shadow. The Prince of Darkness is indeed the embodiment of the Left Hand Path, in that Ahriman is modeled as an Isolate Being independent from the natural order. He exists beyond that veil of light and is immortalized in darkness. Angra Mainyu or Ahriman is the Lord of the Druj[10], which are demons or isolate intelligences (shades) which are as well sorcerers. In traditional Zoroastrian mythology and religious texts, the Druj is horrifying and demonic. In the context of this writing such spirits are models of Antinomian thought and self-deification, and should be viewed in such a manner. While the sorcerer is hidden within the fabric of its own inherent culture, many rites and workings are of the secret and cunning path. One particular essence is that of Ahriman.

Ahriman or Angra Mainyu is essentially a shapeshifting sorcerous principle of magick, who is balanced as both spiritual and physical. In some Zoroastrian tales, Ahriman

---

[9] Yatuk Dinoih translates Witchcraft, and is represented as the religion of Sorcerers, Witches and Wizards. The Bundahishn "Creation" or Knowledge from the Zand - Sacred Books of the East, Oxford, 1897

[10] Druj translates Lie and is symbolized by the Pahlavi books as falsehood. Lie is also associated with the word against the sun, thus symbolizing the shadow or vampyric essence.

first manifested in the world as the Snake who by the element Air, brought darkness into light.

The Left Hand Path in reference to Ahriman is partially on his creation. In some text, Ahriman was not created by Ahura but he possessed an isolate and independent existence, or psyche. Another version of the myth[11], Ahriman first heard his fathers' word, and rip from the womb to greet his father, Zurvan, who replied he was dark and stinking. Ahriman was granted rule for 9,000 years, from which indicated by Will against his father granted the spark which created rebellion.

The form of Ahriman is Draconis, the Black Dragon from which all emerge into their own solitary being, from a Left Hand Path perspective, and fall to subconsciously. Druj is translated LIE as well as connected with Dragon. Those who walk the path of shadows, which is of ecstasy, shall know the fruits of the awakened, perceived sense of self, the "I" of the arcana. The goal of Left Hand Path Sorcery is NOT to become a Shell, but to sharpen, strengthen and develop the individual, isolate consciousness – to be as shadow, as Ahriman itself.

Ahriman or Angra Mainyu created Six archdemons to pervert/awaken mankind. They are Akoman (Aka Manah), Savar (Sauru), Andar (Indra), Nakahed (Naonhaithya), Tairev (Taurvi) and Zairich. These daevas or divs are essential deific masks within the circle of the Yatuk Dinoih, these primal energies represent facets of individual initiation. Aeshma was given the power to govern and control these ArchDaevas, as he united them to direct them in humanity.

The Great Letters and Sigil of Ahriman, known as the Dragon of Darkness, which may be as a word of Ahriman in Avestan, or a illustration which depicts the spirit of darkness.

---

[11] The Zurvanite Myth, The Dawn and Twilight of the Zoroastrianism, R.C. Zaehner, New York, 1961.

The Above Sigil is an Ahriman sigil – within, the Black Dragon and the Three Avestan letters associated with the Yatukih path. The circle always holds letters or sigils which announce the nature of the work – the center is the visualization of Ahriman.

THE PRELIMINARY INVOCATION AND ANNOUNCEMENT OF SELF-IMMOLATION, THE SACRED LUCIFERIAN VISION OF THE INFERNUM.

The circle indicates that it should be made with the system related to the Yatuk Dinoih, the grand awakening of a sleeping religion and initiatory system of Persian Sorcery. Let your circle be cast, to represent the Dragon itself – the very circumference of your being. *Thus a circle is not a protection, rather a gathering place of shadow.* This is the focus point of your sorcery (to en-circle).

    1. Light a black candle on the altar

2. Image of Ahriman or Yatukih Daevas should be adorned on altar.

3. The Evocation Dagger or Black Hilted Knife.

Take the Evocation Dagger, sacred blade of Druj[12] and invoke facing the North, the altar and center of the work.

> "Ahriman, who brings Hesham, who is of Samahe, I stand within the circle of the worm to invoke the mysteries of the ancient source of creation and destruction. From which that you have spoken to me in the sacred dreaming temple, in the Garden of the Arcana of Azothoz, the primal initiator of opposites. I invoke thee! Ahriman, that which opposes the natural order, to become as Alpha Omega itself, as God itself, to create and destroy. Ahriman, who communes with the ancient dead, sleeping and lusting for the living flesh, I invoke thee! Ahriman, from the ruins of the desert, I call you from your place in the darkness. You who marks form from shadows, daemons of the caves of the earth, I invoke thee! To your consort, AZ-JAHI, primal goddess of blood and darkness, who manifests as Lilith and Babalon, come forth, lift your crimson veil and let me taste of your infernal treasures. In the core of your very being shall I shake the foundations of the sacred pillar of Life, absorb its secrets and emerge through the Perfect and illuminated Temple of Darkness! I invoke thee! I shall come forth as an avatar upon earth! Come forth within me!" O maker of the material world, O sacred Druj, I summon thee!"
>
> "Alas, the gates of twilight open before me. The dagger drips the blood of the wretched and weak.

---

[12] Druj is also symbolic of Dragon and snake. The snake is said to speak lies, but those who may listen, wisdom.

> *Would the sacrifice of the howling wolves seek my very soul? Yet, I may brave them, not stopping to witness their fangs inches away from the very soul. Algol itself shall tear through me, yet it is a mirror of my own perfection, being and possibility. I go forth through the Arcana of Dreaming and waking, let Ahriman be my guide of shadows!"*

Lower the knife, turning the blade towards yourself, announcing the desire to raise darkness through your body.

Focus upon your consciousness and what Ahriman represents. In solitude you shall summon and in isolation will the Blackened Flame ignite. Understand that your Words make flesh your desires, so choose your creations carefully. Listen to the voices of the shadows, but more importantly that of your own Mind (**Aka Manah**). In time you will begin working with the NIRANGS and other Avestan inversions in THE BIBLE OF THE ADVERSARY, these will require that you have grown comfortable with methods of sorcery.

Take the time to meditate on the shape shifting qualities of Ahriman. He is known to have taken the form of a Toad, or a Snake, of a Dragon. Animals which were said to be created and are sacred to Ahriman are Wolves, Ants, Serpents, Toads, etc. You may wish to meditate upon changing into each form, allowing by dream to go forth and see as they would see – **RECORD YOUR RESULTS!**

THE DRUJ
The Ritual of Yatukan Sorcery

The religion of the Dregvants (The Followers or People of the Lie) are those who are initiates of Sorcery, or the religion of Ahriman. Such initiation is led by instinctual opposition. It should be kept in mind that within the parameters of psychological evocation, that identification is based upon the success factor of the sorcerer. Witchcraft and Sorcery themselves are based in achievement through identification, counterbalancing restrictive aspects associated with ones own psychological make up. As the gateway of the Magickal Art, we must pass beyond the first definitions, as they are merely gateways, tests from which we may pass through. Each whisper, chant or calling is the elemental control of our surroundings, our own individual universe and vibrations, which create effects accordingly. The Dragon that coils around our brains is the counter point of awakening, from which one aligned; our results of sorcery and magickal workings may double in positive response.

Ahriman, in the ancient Persian religion of Zoroastrianism is the personification of what is called 'The Devil', which is specifically defined as the Daevas which all emerge in darkness. Darkness, keep in mind, is the personification of the void from which we all emerge, it is Chaos and its symbol is the Chaos Sphere.

The workings of this modern grimoire of Yatukan Sorcery are centered on the Sigil of ALGOL, the Chaos Star. It is this mirror which we may project our Will and the Daevas which shall be evoked emerge ultimately through this mirror.

While the ALGOL sphere is not Zoroastrian, it holds a center in the focus of darkness. The use of Art to express the 'Matter' or materialization of the Daevas is also beneficial to the Artist. It was said that Ahriman brought Smoke to Fire, to if outdoors, perform invocations with fire and smoke.

Visualize Ahriman and such spirits in the smoke coming from the flames.

The Seven Archdemons of Yatukan Sorcery are the centers of antinomian advancement, from which the sorcerer may advance by their own centers of evocation and invocation. Approach these forces carefully, but boldly. The ultimate test of awakening is to invoke the Daevas from without the protection circle, in the evocation circle itself. Absorb them - let them become you. This is the way to know of your true possibility of becoming.

The Seven Archdemons are as follows:

AKA MANAH (Akoman, the Evil Mind)

INDRA (Andar, Dev of the Black Flame)

SAURU (Savar, the Lord of Daevas or Devs, corresponds with the Medieval and Gnostic Belial, the Lord of the Earth)

TAURVI (Tairev, a dev of rebellion)

ZAIRITSHA (Zairich is a dev of poison, used as a spirit of herbalism or of cursing)

NAONHAITHYA (Naikiyas, a dev of antinomian thought, rebellion, discontent, desire)

AESHMA (Asmodeus the demon of the wounding spear)

It should be noted as well that Asmodeus is of essentially Persian origin, known as Acshma (Demon of the Wounding Spear). The name Ashmedai emerged from Hebrew and Latin and Asmodeus once was an Angel of the Seraphim, from which he fell with Lucifer or Ahriman. Jewish lore presents Asmodeus as a child of Tubal Cain and Naamah, the demon queen and former bride of Satan. The gnosis achieved through invocation with Aeshma will reveal by inspiration the foundations of the Holy law and why it was trespassed by Ahriman and the Seven Daevas. A hint to be given to the reader is that by moving against the current of laws within a belief structure lead to the strengthening of the individual, the birth of a God or Goddess. This force is essential in the advancement of the universe, often misunderstood in modern belief structures commonly understood as 'morals' in the era of social comprehension. Evoke and Invoke the mysteries from which the sorcerer may awaken their own semblance of possibility. Our forms shall be many, from which shall reflect in the mirror of Algol.

The sigil of Yatukan Sorcery in a modern context is:

ALGOL – A word which derives from the Arabic Al Ra's al Ghul, Al-Ghul, or Ri'B al Ohill, which is translated "The Demon's Head". Algol was in Hebrew known as Rosh ha Shaitan, or "Satan's Head", as some traditions have referred to Algol as the Head of Lilith. The Chinese called Algol Tseih She, which is "Piled up corpses" and was considered a violent, dangerous star due to its changing vivid colors. On some 17th century maps Algol was labeled, "The Specter's Head". Algol upon some research has indicated that possibility Three stars which are an eclipsing binary, which may explain some of the rapid color change. Some writers have connected Algol with the Egyptian Khu, or spirit. The Khu is considered a shadow spirit which feeds on other shades of the dead. In reference to the writings and initiatory symbolism of Michael W. Ford, ALGOL is the sigillized in one form as a Chaos Star with an Averse Pentagram in the center. The Pentagram refers to the Eye of Set, timeless and divine, godlike and independent. The Chaos Star is destruction, Change and power – all of which emerges from the Eye of Shaitan, or Set. It is this Chaos which then brings Order. ALGOL is the mirror of the sorcerer, one who may enter and reside in the pulsing eye of blackened flame. There are Eight God Forms which are manifested from the Center of the Chaos Star – within are Five Daemon Guardians of the

Five Worlds within Hell, Helan and all are interconnected with the Center Force of Spirit of the Prince of Darkness.

As mentioned previously, the Sigil or Eye of Algol is that of the Fallen Seraphim, the angels which dove the abyss to taste the knowledge and become as the dragon's spirit, the serpent of the garden. Use the Mirror of the Adepts to isolate consciousness, and to place the Daevas of your summoning through, which may emerge for your desired working when the gnosis of the Temple is achieved.

When working with the Chaos Sphere, realize that in a historical sense the original chaos sigil was a symbol of God and Spirit. This proves essential in the understanding of moving past ideas which present a moralistic challenge to the sorcerer. Moving past each symbol is essential in advancing ones own natural abilities to magickal awakening. In Mesopotamia the Chaos Star first appeared in the Temples, dating around 3000 B.C. making it one of the earliest magical symbols. One may use the Algol sigil to call forth the Daemons of the abyss and use the magickal mirror to send them back. The Chaos Sphere is essential in magickal work pertaining to evocation and projecting desires. One may use the Chaos Sphere as also a tool to absorb anothers attack, causing to spell to return to the maker. This would enable the fetish they use to attack you as a means of their own torment, and will thus be used against them. The only remedy for such is for the creator to destroy the fetish used to curse you, or if returned unknown, will slowly feed from the aggressor's astral body until sickness occurs. It is always suggested for the sorcerer to send back this curse unknowingly to the aggressor, as it will lead to a healthy destruction of the individual. If the curse is returned to the individual, you will have used the force of your will and the magickal mirror of the Algol Sphere to do such, thus you may evoke certain Yatukan daemons to move through the mirror and feast from the aggressor. The experienced Sorcerer will be able to use divination methods regarding the Algol Sphere to discover happens around him or her. Such hidden methods make a powerful background to one who practices Witchcraft, especially within the Wiccan areas. While the Witch is experienced in the rituals of Wicca or Witchcraft, the hidden dark elements make the sorcerer much more powerful than initially detected. Many experienced witches will be able to sense what is below the surface, however the witch in question may be able to conceal such effects as well.

THE EVOCATION CIRCLE:

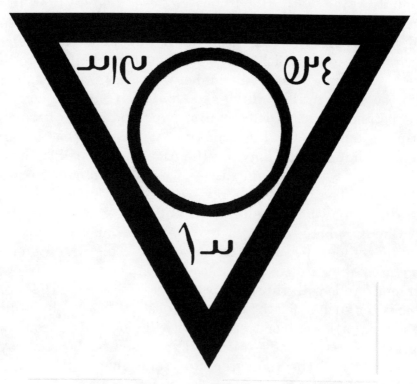

ABOVE: The Yatukih Evocation Triangle.

INSTRUCTIONS FOR USING THE TRIANGLE TO CONSTRAIN SPIRITS:

1. Place the sigil of the spirit into the circle within the triangle. This will be the focus point of your ritual. Do not enter this circle by any means unless you will call it within youself (this is not recommended for beginners).

2. During the evocation, visualize the spirit taking form. You may place a black mirror behind the triangle and you may notice shapes taking form.

3. While evoking, some Luciferians enter the circle to call inward the spirit, this may complicate the process. You must be strong enough to overmaster, consume and absorb the spirit into your psyche or it may cause you problems. Be cautious. This increases the magical power of the Luciferian each time this is performed.

4. If you cut yourself in the rite to offer your own blood, then you will enter the circle. There will be a connection – the spirit will manifest from your own blood. A burnt offering such as nails, skin, hair or such will strengthen the rite.

Concerning Sacrifice

When summoning/binding the Daevas and Druj of the Yatuk Dinoih, it is essential to offer a sacrifice of Hair, Nails or spittle to them. In Zoroastrian lore, it is a sacrifice to throw hair, nails or any such body fluid in a hole or crack where sun does not reach. When working, especially outside if you are able to create a hole or use a crack near some rocks or otherwise. Anything which is taken from man or woman, hair, etc and cast down is considered unclean and something demons attach to.

In the VENDIDAD, reference is made to the act of feeding Druj, knowingly or unknowingly, and thus warns against it.

"Zarathushtra asked Ahura Mazda: 'O Ahura Mazda, most beneficent Spirit, Maker of the material world, thou Holy One! Which is the most deadly deed whereby a man offers up a sacrifice to the Daevas?

Ahura Mazda answered: 'It is when a man here below, combing his hair or shaving it off, or paring off his nails, drops them in a hole or in a crack 'Then by this transgression of the rites, Daevas are produced in the earth" -VENDIDAD, Fargard 17

THE RITUAL OF SORCERY

Warning – Do not attempt this ritual if you or any participant has any history of mental problems, as this will surely lead to a less than pleasant result. The forces evoked are indeed real and should be approached seriously. The author and publisher accept no responsibility for the use of this book. Use caution and you have been warned.

ITEMS REQUIRED:

Black Candles

Evocation Dagger

Chalice

Wand

Evocation Triangle with Sigil of Spirit

Charcoal and burner for offering

CALLING OF THE SHADOW -

Under the stars which emerge of AZ, from the tombs of the mighty dead, I do call and summon thee, from which I am the shadow of form, black and hungered for the nourishment of the living shade. Andar under thy cloak of hidden darkness, to me! Awaken to my rite:

THE SACRIFICE

Offer now some of your own hair, nails, spittle or sexual sacrifice in the designated hole or crack while chanting:

"By Paitisha and Hesham I offer this to thee, for I am Dregvantem, and Daevayasnanam whose word is Druj. Take my sacrifice of my life force and give back your blessings and assistance, for we are one and the same. I feed the shadows to expand the darkness. O Mazainya Daevas! These nails I announce and consecrate unto thee, spirits of darkness. May they be for thee so manyknives and spears, so many bows and falcon-winged arrows and so many weapons against the Sheep of the Rightious!"

The sorcerer would take a small bit of hair, or nail or something from his or her and drop in a hole or crack while uttering the chant of sacrifice, this is an affirmation of aligning the self with the Yatuvidah current and the supposed creation of demons in the earth. *The religious work of a Yatus, or Luciferian, is to take previously cleaned human bones and wash them in water to which you shall drink ritualistically, feeds the Druj and envenoms the sorcerer as being at one with the faith he or she develops.*

THE SUMMONING OF AHRIMAN

FACE THE ALTAR WHILE RECITING:

ZAZAS ZAZAS NASATANADA ZAZAS

I summon thee, Arimanius, Armiluss,

Come thou forth from thy dire mansion

Ensorcel me in shades and by dream – BECOME!

By flame and lightening, the Darkness of the Abyss

I seek to ride the Dragon Azi Dahaka,

Join in flesh the Scarlet Whore, Ruha-Az,

That by wolf and serpent shall ride her flesh

Manifest through thy summoner, enfleshed Akhtya

And thy Summoned manifest as You

By the Circle Dance against the Sun DRUJ arise!

Praise unto Ahriman, whose form may be the Toad – the Gateway to the Devil's Mysteries

Praise unto Ahriman, who drinks the blood of wolves and from shadow creates their perception – the shades may enter the mind of darkness to drink deep of the blood of the moon.

Ahriman, by the Dragon encircle me!

Ahriman by the Wolf enflesh in me!

Ahriman by Khrafstras guide me!

Arimanius, Andar, so it is done!

A PRAYER OF AHRIMAN
FACE THE ALTAR AND RECITE:

O' Dragon who rushes from the North,

O Serpent Druj of Darkness, Smoke, Cold and Noxious Heat, I summon thee

In Kalch (Filth) I call thee, by the Averse Ways of Midnight and Midday

Of Tauromat, who is the Druj of Rebellion

Below me, Nasai (Dead Matter) which strengthens my spirit – Kundak who shall carry me to the Sabbat and upon the Earth in Dreaming Flesh, Akoman Guide me!

O Wolf Druj Ahriman I Invoke thee....Maghaaman...Izzadraana!

A Sacred Hymn to Darkness:

And to that one of beings (of daevayasnanam) whose superior in the becoming of Akoman, of Ahriman, who knows and who gives Daevodata, whose Yatus and Parikas do we become as, who shall we worship ourselves through!

Pihsrow ew od sgnieb elamef dna elam esohw elamef lla fo esoht dna ssnsuoethgir sih morf dna, swonk adzam aruha ecifircas eht ni roirepus esohw sgnieb foe no that dna!

(Let a small drop of spittle hit the candle or touch the flame with spit on your finger or hand)

THE EVOCATION AND CONSTRAINT

Being the summoning and controlling of the forces of the earth, the sorcerer visualizes the beast taking form within the circle, the letters at the Three Points of the Circle are the deific gathering of the elements of Ahriman, the Avestan letters spelling out Ahriman. The sorcerer or witch will then invoke this force within by a symbolic entering of the triangle and circle, allowing possession of the Prince of Darkness as it shall be made manifest through the psyche of the practitioner. This ritual is not the surrendering of the individual being, rather the empowerment and encircling of it – Ahriman being a fleshed out deific power made real by the Yatuvidah his/herself.

Facing the circle of evocation, focusing on the Daeva or Spirit-

"Zazasta Unozono" (Recite Nine Times)

"Rush to me, Daevas and Druj of shadow and blackened earth, those who nourish the corpse, who guide the insects and slithering things, messengers of life beyond the veil of death's arms. Come forth from the depths of the raging dark world of hell, encircle me and manifest in this Circle. By the Three points of Ahriman, who with Akoman is the Eye in the Darkness which empowers the isolate soul!

Daevas, Gather now at the head of Arezura – I open now the gates of Hell to hear my calls – I am thy messenger upon earth, move up and ascend into this circle!

Angra Mainyu, father of the Daevas of which I am, I evoke thee!

Andar, Shadow of Umbra and Nocturnal Sight, Bring the Blackened Flame!

Savar Lord of Druj and Daeva, I evoke thee forth!

Akatasha Daeva, I summon thee!

Naunghaithya the Daeva, I evoke thee unto this Circle!

Zairich and Taprev I Summon thee by the Ghost Ways – Arise!

Buiti the Daeva, sender of Ahriman's wishes I summon thee!

Kasvi the Daeva, I evoke thee!

Aeshma, Daeva of the Murdering Spear I evoke thee!

As I enter this circle I invoke the Daeva and Druj known as Paitisha, who is perfect in darkness – the Dragon Within!

"Arimznusta" Recite Three times, each time envisioning darkness forming into a great beast within the circle.

"Izzadrana" – Vibrate Nine times and enter by imagination or physically into the circle. If circle is too small, place thy left hand in the circle.

Great manifestation of the Abyss, from which all emerges, I do summon thee forth. By the names INDRA, SAURU, TAURVI, AESHMA, ZAIRITSHA, NAONHAITHYA and AKA MANAH come forth! By Iklitu shall you come forth, By Iklitu shall you emerge from by my Will, Arise O Azhish, come Druj, come Daeva for I am of dragvantem, the path against all others!

The Charge -
Point Evocation Dagger

Daeva (name),

As I touch thee with this Dagger, forged of the Fire of the Dahakem, do manifest. I name and call you by Zakaru! By Ahriman's Kiss do I conjure thee and bring thee into this space, bring the shadows to encircle me in the ecstasy of the serpent.

I do charge thee to hear my voice, which is that which gives you life, it is my Will for you to manifest now! I am Daevayasnanam, who becomes in the circle of Druj! I encircle you, Alalu, remain, Alalu, manifest, Alalu, by my Will.

The Constraint -

Daeva, Appear before me in this circle, from which I have given thee form and substance. I do command thee to appear in the form which I desire, do come forth as my friend, great shade of ancestral vision. By the oath of the shadow born, Arimanius! Ahazu, Ahazu, Ahazu!! By samahe, that which we create from, that which drives us, that of which the Dragon coils, that which the Worm awakens from, remain here!

Ask now which you seek with the Daemon, and upon obtaining this information, thank it and banish/close circle. The optional ending is far more dangerous, yet offers greater rewards. Proceed with caution.

"TAKE NOW THIS BURNT OFFERING – I CLOSE THE GATES!"

THE WITCHES SABBAT

Dreams have long been considered images of the subconscious; what lies within the mind. In Magick dreams can be a powerful initiatory tool, if focused upon in a positive and conductive manner may provide excellent self-developmental areas of being. The Witches Sabbat may be conducted in dreaming avenues, if the magician so desires. The model of the Witches Sabbat in a dreaming sense should start with a visualization of the Crossroads. The Crossroads have for long been considered a place of great magickal power. It is the place of Hecate, the Triple Goddess which is the gathering of shades and ghosts; many have evoked her there in the crossroads. It is also the place of where Faust summoned Mephistopheles, who came forth from the forest before him. The Crossroads is the place where you visualize and focus your mind towards before sleep – you may also visualize and X or a + as the meeting place of the Dreaming Sabbat.

The imagination is the ultimate key of the Black Magician or Sorcerer who seeks to go forth to the Sabbat – it is the vehicle of self-assumption of deific forms or masks of lycanthropy. When preparing for the Dream Sabbat, decorate your temple or sleeping area in accordance with that which reminds you of a Sabbat – images from old grimoires, sigils, demonic images, masks or other elements which aid the Working. The most important however is the control of the mind. Sit comfortably before and clear all thoughts. Begin a slow chant which you know that 'activates' the imagination towards the Sabbat.

Use the Five Senses to activate and aid this transformative 'in-between' state – hearing, sight, smell, touch and taste. Have some pleasant Sabbat incense and perfect lighting in place, have sigils and images which invoke this place in the mind. Your goal is to align the senses with the focus of the Going forth by Night – that is by harmony with the Willed choice of desire. Preparing for the Sabbat by decorating and proper self-alignment creates a heightened inner excitement for the initiatory act itself – thus allowing the success to occur, a seeming self-permission!

The Sabbat is a subjective experience, from which you are alone and surrounded by the shades and familiars of your own design. Early on you will discover during waking hours elements of yourself you wish to change and common traits or self-associations or perceptions you will slowly understand through the process of change. Be accepting and use this as a permission to become! The Witches Sabbat is used for many purposes – it is for self-deification, exploration, shape shifting and a heightened gnosis state – it breaks through mystery and reveals a new perception, you become "like" the Devil or "Adversary", you grow close to Hecate and Lilith, and you gain a more direct focus of Magickal Will. The Sabbat is also used for Spells and Sexual Workings as well – a Sabbat experience with a partner is perhaps one of the most ecstasy inducing acts that can be shared by two people – or more if that is your "bag". The Sabbat may also be used to curse and bless, all which spirals and acts as a spring – the very magickal principle the Staota is in the Second Edition of Yatuk Dinoih. Do not invite the initiated into the Circle of the Witches Sabbat, for the Ensorcelment of Cain will devour them and curse them in whole. Such an experience if ever shared must be between two understanding initiates – self-initiated or otherwise. Remember, the Sabbat goes back to the Antinomianian principle of Luciferian self-deification. It is a path of knowledge through clarity – this clarity is discovered by those who are focused on moving past mystery, a major point of the beginning of what lies hidden.

Luciferian Magick as within the model of the Witches Sabbat proves a challenging and darksome journey wherein the initiate drinks deep from the Skull Cup filled with the venom'd blood of Seth-an, who then eats of the Flesh of Abel and whose blood is offered to his own Angel-Demon, the very essence and representation of the Great Work itself.

The Sabbat as being a dual participation of both dreaming and ceremonial/solitary ritual is represented as the fleshing of desire and belief, wherein the arcana of Cain is revealed to the intiate, where there is no further difference between the Great Whore Lilith-Az and Samael as the Adversary, all are one through the expanding and deification of the magician. In summary the witch becomes a vessel and expression of Ahriman and his Bride, thus the Circle of Lucifer is complete and the casting has brought forth Cain, thus the initiate is the first of Witch Blood and the Gnosis of Shadow and Light.

In "Ecstasies: Deciphering the Witches Sabbat" by Carlo Ginzburg, he describes one rite which the attributes mentioned hold resonance with not only present practice, but ancient practice as well. "the devil appeared to them in the shape of a black animal – sometimes a bear, sometimes a ram. After having renounced God, faith, baptism and the Church" and goes on to described horrific rites of cursing. Another section mentions witches wearing the skin of wolves to transform themselves. This is a process of atavistic resurgence and is still practiced today, while in the affirmation of the Devil is a deeper association to self-deification and the recognition of the conscious mind; the lycanthropy practiced is the atavistic summoning of the Therion – shades within the body and mind.

When using the Waking Sabbat rite for spell casting or sorcery, you will want to have a clear idea of what you want to achieve. You will also want to create or adopt a sigil which holds connection to the goal – or it may represent the desire of the spell. You may also use a Mantra or phrase which holds significance to the same. As you perform the rite, with the decorated chamber or even in the woods, envision the demons and familiars in your company and the spirits carrying your Will to become Flesh. As your rite comes to a climax, loose all desire in the sigil at the moment of exhaustion. If you have a sigil for the working, destroy it and forget it – the rite should then be enjoyed as a "walking in the crossroads" or in-between worlds.

The Spell of Going forth as a crow or owl
- Recite three times before sleep

I shall go into a crow
With sorrow sigh and mickle care
And I shall go in the Devil's name
Ay while I come home again

The Spell of Returning to the Flesh
-Recite three times

Owl, Owl, Devil send thee care
I am in an Owl's likeness just now
But I shall be in a wo(mans) likeness even now

The Spell of Changing into a Cat
– Recite three times

I shall go into a cat
With sorrow and sigh and a black sigh
And I shall go in the Devil's name
Ay while I come home again

THE GATES OF AREZURA

This is a ritual from which the initiate opens the gates of hell that is the meeting place of sorcerers and witches – those who travel into the darkness and flame of the Sabbat. The Gates of Arezura is the initiatory point of which "I" is revealed and may become. You will realize your goals, your potentials and weaknesses to emerge to one who is becoming as Ahriman.

As Ahriman is a form of the Adversary in a primal sense, the darkness of being is to be explored and perceived as an extension of self. The aspect of Ahriman is as half-beast, werewolf type vampyre from. Ahriman is a spirit of darkness, whom resides in the depths of the subconscious – the Gates of Arezura. One should focus on encircling the self in these shadows, which are revealed by the Work itself. The essence of Yatus/Yatuk is the mysteries of sorcery within the self, the keys to the spirit of man. One works this type of considered Dangerous Black Magick as the self-transformation through the image of the Adversary. Akhtya is the sorcerer on earth who drinks of the graal of Ahriman and Az, serpent and wolf. This inversion leads to the strengthening of self under the activity of encircling belief into tangible form.

One should prepare for the ritual of Arezura by a deep introspection, becoming aware of what you wish to achieve and become. You master the self through the entry and exploration of the Gates of Hell – it is also the meeting place of sorcerers, witches and Daevas (demons) of the fiery darkness. It is where Dreams become Flesh.

THE INVOCATION – Facing the North, the direction of Arezura-

I summon thee, Gateway of Arezura – that you shall open forth to me-

Hail unto thee Ahriman, Lord of Flame and Shadow

Dweller in the dark places of the Earth

Lord and Creator of Wolves, serpents and toads...

As the Night comes forth, you shall attend through me..

I open these gates as the gathering place of the dream,

That in 8 nights shall I become in Shadow the reflection of the 8 Midday journeys to the Sun-

That the Bornless Fire exists in the Eyes of those who walk this path

Ahriman, Arimanius – Acsend through me!

You, summoned unto me – wolf shadow, flyer of night –

I am in flesh Akhtya, encircling my being in the sacred letters of Yatuk-Dinoih

Open now the gates of Arezura and behold the flames of the Djinn, our creative fire of becoming...by the ancient words of Power-

Zazas, Zazas Nasatanada Zazas!

ENCIRCLING THE SPIRIT – ENTERING THE GATES

I summon thee, behold and hail thee – VIZARESH, Guardian of the Gates – Those who have recognized the sacred flame of my being – I enter these gates unto the kingdom of shadow and sorcerous knowledge.

In the name of Ahriman, I do encircle my being – against the Sun, Against the Moon do I walk. In opposition to Order – by this ecstasy do I bask in Chaos – Mummu – Algol – To create Order I reside in the Eye of Darkness

I summon and bind thee – shades of Ahriman..Encircle me!

AZI-DAHAKA – Storm Demon, King with twin Serpents unto your shoulders – whom Ahriman hath Kissed and Wisdom emerges – Serpent of Three Heads, Eyes of Hekate, come forth. Those who summon against me will only strengthen me!

ANDAR- Guardian of the Black Flame, I summon thee! Wraith of the Void of Arezura – TO ME – TO ME!

TAROMAT – *Spirit of Rebellion come forth unto me! TO ME! TO ME!*

ASTWIHAD – Vampyre and Night Shade, whom I rest beside in Darkness – Whom I fly with in dreaming flesh, encircle me!

BUITI – Ahriman's hammer and knife – Those who summon against me shall taste thy blades of burning metal in dreams!

KUNDAK – Flying Nightmare come forth unto me!

As you enter the gates, envision each demon and what they represent to you. The Gates of Arezura is a mirror of yourself, a new level of coming into being. You have passed the hidden place, a new initiation is presented to you. Drink from this cup of Serpent wisdom.

EMERGING FROM THE GATES (CLOSING THE RITE)-

As I strengthen myself in flame and shadow of my sorceries, I do understand who and what I am and I know what I wish to become. In opposition I am of the Sun and the Moon. Al-Dajjal and Lilith-born.

I am wolf and bat, in dreams I may walk in secrecy, by Kunda – who is drunk from the blood of Sheep I become!

As I stand at the Head of Arezura – I enter in flesh the material world

To manifest my desires – to become, advance and change the world according to my Will

By ZAZAS I become

By ZAZAS I am Always

By Nasatanada In Opposition I become

By Zazas I change the World by my Will

SO IT IS DONE

APPENDIX: LEGACY OF THE LEFT HAND PATH

Diabolica

The Satanic Bible by Anton Szandor LaVey

NAOS by the Order of the Nine Angles

The Book of Black Magic by Arthur Edward Waite

Book of the Witch Moon, Luciferian Witchcraft, Bible of the Adversary, Vampire Gate, First Book of Luciferian Tarot by the present author

Ancient, Mythological

Bundahishn Zoroastrian cosmology

    Greater Bundahishn

    Denkard

    Selections of Zadspram

The Sufis by Idries Shah

Babylonian Magic and Sorcery by Leonard W. King, M.A.

The Book of Lilith by Barbara Black Koltuv, Ph.D

The Leyden Papyrus Edited by F.Ll. Griffith & Herbert

Egyptian Magic by E.A. Wallis Budge

The Gods of the Egyptians by E.A. Wallis Budge

Traditional, Historical, Classical

Magick in Theory and Practice by Aleister Crowley

The Goetia translated by S.L. MacGregor Mathers and Aleister Crowley

WITCHA – A Book of Cunning by Nathaniel J. Harris

Initiation into Hermetics by Franz Bardon

A History of Secret Societies by Arkon Daraul

Modern, Post-Modern and Beyond

Liber Kaos, Liber Null/Psychonaut by Peter Carroll

Practical Sigil Magick by Frater UD

My Life with the Spirits by Don Milo Duquette

GLOSSARY

Ahriman [Avestan/Pahlavi] – The Prince of Darkness in Zoroastrian Religion. Ahriman is considered one brother created by Zurvan and was the opposing force to Ohura Mazda. Ahriman is also known as Angra Mainyu, an older title derived from Angra Mainyu, being the "evil" or averse spirit. Ahriman is a sorcerer who achieved a means of immortality and power over darkness and shadow. One who creates his desire in flesh. In relation to the sorcerer or practitioner of Yatuk-Dinoih, the individual seeks by developing their own system of sorcery, to become like Ahriman, just as did Akht-Jadu in the Zoroastrian tales. Ahriman is called the Great Serpent or Dragon, whose spirit is a shapeshifter and tester of flesh and mind. It was considered in some Zoroastrian tales that Ahriman and the Daevas, his angels, ecisted between the earth and the fixed stars, which would be essentially of the element Air (much like Lucifer his later identification). In creation myths, Ahriman first saw light and sprang into the air in the form of a great snake, that the heavens were shattered as he brought darkness into light.

Ahrimanic Yoga – Achieving control and command over the body. Each ArchDaeva is representative of each Chakra and such are points of specific power in the body. Ahrimanic Yoga represents disunion with the universe, as opposed to union from a Buddhist view.

Akha [Avestan/Pahlavi] - Avestan, meaning evil. In the context of Liber HVHI and Luciferian Witchcraft, it is a term signifying the antinomian path.

Akho [Avestan/Pahlavi] – From the Avestan "akha" meaning "evil", Akho is mentioned in the Denkard as a word representing a "current" of averse energy or evil, through which one aligning their thoughts in possessing spiritual independence, antinomianism and self-deification one may reach into the spirit of Ahriman. This supports the initatory foundation of the Luciferian path itself – the Adept prepares to become like the Adversary his or her self, based on their own unique path.

Akht [Avestan/Pahlavi] – The Sorcerer who was the embodiment of the Yatus, the demonic forces of Ahriman. Akht-Jadu or Kabed-us-spae as he was called was mentioned in Matigan-I Yosht-I Fryan. Akhtya was the founder and member of the Yatus, a coven of 'demons' and sorcerers who wandered Persia, practicing and developing sorcery. The name Akht itself means 'evil', 'filth' and 'pestilence', thus relates to the initiatory nature of Akhti as a sorcerer of the Adversary, by the darkness shall he come into light. Akhtya or Azyta is thus considered a symbol of the Zanda, which is an Apostle or Priest of Ahriman.

ALGOL – A word which derives from the Arabic Al Ra's al Ghul, Al-Ghul, or Ri'B al Ohill, which is translated "The Demon's Head". Algol was in Hebrew known as Rosh ha Shaitan, or "Satan's Head", as some traditions have referred to Algol as the Head of Lilith. The Chinese called Algol Tseih She, which is "Piled up corpses" and was considered a violent, dangerous star due to its changing vivid colors. On some 17th century maps Algol was labeled, "The Specter's Head". Algol upon some research has indicated that possibility Three stars which are an eclipsing binary, which may explain some of the rapid color change. Some writers have connected Algol with the Egyptian Khu, or spirit. The Khu is considered a shadow spirit which feeds on other shades of the dead. In reference to the writings and initiatory symbolism of Michael W. Ford, ALGOL is the sigillized in one form as a Chaos Star with an Averse Pentagram in the center. The Pentagram refers to the Eye of Set, timeless and divine, godlike and independent. The Chaos Star is destruction, Change and power – all of which emerges from the Eye of Shaitan, or Set. It is this Chaos which then brings Order. ALGOL is the mirror of the sorcerer, one who may enter and reside in the pulsing eye of blackened flame.

Arezura [Avestan/Pahlavi] – Arezurahe griva (Arezura) in the Bundahishin is called "a mount at the gate of hell, whence the demons rush forth". Arezura is the gate to hell in the Alburz mountain range in present day Iran. The North is traditionally the seat of Ahriman, wherein the cold winds may blow forth. Arezura from an initiatory perspective is the subconscious, the place where sorcerers may gather and grow in their arts, by encircling and manifesting their desire. M.N. Dallah wrote in "The History of Zoroastrianism" concerning a connection with demons holding mastery over the earth, their ability to sink below the earth and that such demons around the time of Zoroaster walked the earth in human form. In the Denkard, it is described that one who becomes a vessel for the "evil religion" becomes physically an abode for "Unholy Demons" or Daevas. One grows aligned to Arezura spiritually by practicing with discipline the path of Daeva-yasna or Yatukih sorcery. Arezur or Arzur is the name of an early Son of Ahriman who killed the First man.

ASANA – Posture relating to the practice of Yoga. In reference to the Luciferian Path, posture is anything which is steady or consistent. There is no defined posture in Ahrimanic Yoga, although there are suggestions.

ATAVISM – A beast-like subconscious memory of knowledge, a pre-human aspect of the subconscious –the serpent, crocodile or other reptilian form. Atavisms are often latent power points in the mind.

ASTOVIDAD [Avestan/Pahlavi] – The demon of darkness who is utilized as a godform for the Vampyre Magickian in terror or atavistic feeding rituals. Astovidad is a demon of death, who has great powers given to him by Ahriman. He is called the Evil Flyer.

AZ [Avestan/Pahlavi] – Called 'Concupiscence', Az is represented as Primal Sexual Hunger, that which eventually devours all things. Az is also related to menstruation (The KISS of Ahriman causes menstruation in women) and is a destroyer through chaos. Az was connected with Sexual Hunger but also religious doubt, which relates her to a Luciferian Spirit who broke the chains of dogma by the Black Light, the torch of self-perception of being. Az also represents Lilith as the Goddess of the Beasts of the Earth, the very mother of demons and sorcerous beings. Az was said to be created in the Zurvan myth as a black substance like Coal, which would devour all creation, manifesting her as a vampyric being.

Azazel [Hebrew]– The First Angel who brought the Black Flame of being to humanity. Azazel was the Lord of Djinn and was said to be made of Fire in Islamic lore. Azazel refused to bow before the clay of Adam, saying that it was profane. He was cast from heaven to earth and was indeed the first independent spirit, the initiator of individual and antinomian thought. Azazel was later related to the Watchers, the Hebrew Goat Demon God and Shaitan. Azazel is a name of Lucifer, who is the solar aspect of the Dragon, the Bringer of Light.

Azhi [Avestan/Pahlavi] – Serpent, snake

Azhi Dahaka [Avestan/Pahlavi] – The son of Angra Mainyu/Ahriman. Azhi Dahaka as the 'Storm Fiend' has six eyes, three heads and three pairs of fangs. In human form, he was Zohak, an ancient Babylonian/Scythian/Assyrian King or Shah, who according to Zoroastrian mythology, was transformed into the immortal storm fiend by a pact with Ahriman. Azhi Dahaka is said to be filled with serpents, scorpions, toads and other insects and reptiles.

AZOTHOZ – A sigillic word formula which represent the Golden Dawn definition of the Beginning and End, Alpha and Omega. Azothoz is a reversed form which is a symbol and glyph of the Adversary, Shaitan/Set and Lilith. This is a word which signifies self-initiation and the power which is illuminated by the Black Flame within.

Bevarasp [Avestan/Pahlavi] – Myraid of Horses, meaning also Ten Plagues on humanity. This is a name of Azhi Dahaka or Zohak.

Black Flame – The Gift of Shaitan/Set, being individual perception and deific consciousness. The Black Flame or Black Light of Iblis is the gift of individual awakening which separates the magician from the natural universe, being an Antinomian gift of Luciferian perception. The Black Flame is strengthened by the initiation of the Black Adept, who is able to balance a spiritual path with the physical world.

Black Magick – The practice of Antinomian and self-focused transformation, self-deification and the obtainment of knowledge and wisdom. Black Magick in itself does not denote harm or wrongdoing to others, rather describes "black" as considered to the Arabic root word FHM, charcoal, black and wisdom. Black is thus the color of hidden knowledge. Magick is to ascend and become, by Willed focus and direction.

Cain – The Antinomian nomad and Sorcerer who was the spiritual offspring of Samael (the Black Dragon) and Lilith (Red Dragon/the mother of demons) through the body of Eve in Biblical lore. Cain was said to have been the initiate of the Caul, and through his first step on the Left Hand Path (Antinomian practice) he is the initiator of the sorcerer and witch. Cain is also the Black Smith who sparks the Black Flame in the mind of the initiate. Tubal-Cain is the Baphometic Daemon which is the enfleshed archetype of Azal'ucel, or Lucifer/Samael, the Dragon and Peacock Angel.

Daeva [Avestan/Pahlavi] – demons, those who are children of Ahriman and Az. Daeva also makes reference to "Spirit" of Ahriman, those who have walked the path of the serpent, i.e. antinomianism or the left hand path.

Daeva Yasna [Avestan/Pahlavi] – Demon (Daeva) Worship (Yasna), meaning the Yatukih path of Satanism, that is; the separation from the natural order, by the workings of rituals and discipline – oriented mental/physical workings, becoming a body of darkness and light, a Daeva who is continually expanding consciousness and becoming something new. The term does not reflect the theistic worship or knee bending towards an exterior force, rather a Willed direction of self-advancement by transformation. Daeva represents a "mask" of power, specifically to perceived energies.

Dregvant [Avestan/Pahlavi] – In historical Zoroastrian lore, a person embodied with Druj, the spirit of darkness. Druj is refered as both feminine and masculine, thus is an initiatory term relating to the foremost union of Ahriman and Az, the blackened matter and fiery darkness of his bride. A Dregvant is a Yatu or initiate of the Daeva-Yasna.

Druj [Avestan/Pahlavi] – "Lie" referring to demons, feminine and masculine. The later derived term is interestingly enough the old Persian "Draug", meaning also "Lie" and is held connected to "Serpent", "Snake" or "Dragon" (i.e. Worm). Druj is a title representing antinomian power in a personage, a daeva in flesh.

Evil Eye – In the old Gathic writings, the Evil Eye is considered a power of the Daeva and Druj, meaning the power to cause death, oppression and sickness. In a modern sense, the Evil Eye represents the window to the Soul or Spirit itself, not merely as a negative but equally so a positive. The Eye of the Yatu is the commanding presence which is a form of spell casting, to focus the Will itself on the desired goal, to achieve a result. Many Daevas are directly related to the Evil Eye, thus is as well a symbol of Ahriman.

Ghanamino [Avestan/Pahlavi] – Name of Ahriman or Angra Mainyu, spelling from the Denkard. Occuring also as Ganamino and Akundag (*from Manichaean texts*).

HVHI – Reverse of IHVH, the name of God in Cabalism. HVHI is the name of Samael and Lilith, the Adversary – the very name of darkness manifest.

Jahi [Avestan/Pahlavi] – The companions/concubines of the Yatu. An alternative spelling of Jeh.

Jeh [Avestan/Pahlavi] – A manifestation of the Whore, AZ in Zoroastrian lore. Jeh is a consort of Ahriman, the Sorcerous Daemon of shadow and darkness. It was she who awoke Ahriman from his great slumber, that which no other sorcerer, wizard, witch or demon could do. Jeh-AZ is the sexual and inspiration drive which causes movement, friction and change. Jeh and Az represent predatory spirituality, the hunger for continued existence.

Khrafstra [Avestan/Pahlavi] – Beast, representing a dev (demon) on earth, Scorpion, wolf, fly, bat, serpent, lizard, toad and any creation of Ahriman.

Left Hand Path – The Antinomian (*against the current, natural order*) path which leads through self-deification (godhood). LHP signifies that humanity has an intellect which is separate from the natural order, thus in theory and practice may move forward with seeking the mastery of the spirits (referring to the elements of the self) and controlled direction in a positive area of ones own life – the difference between RHP is they seek union with the universe, nirvana and bliss. The LHP seeks disunion to grow in perception and being, strength and the power of an awakened mind. The Left Hand Path from the Sanskrit Vama Marga, meaning 'Left Way', symbolizes a path astray all others, subjective only to itself. To truly walk upon the Left Hand Path, one must strive to break all personal taboos and gain knowledge and power from this averse way, thus expand power accordingly.

Lilith [Hebrew]– The Goddess of Witchcraft, Magick and Sorcery. Lilith was the first wife of Adam who refused to be submission and joined with the shadows and demonic spirits in the deserts. Lilith was also said to be the spiritual mother of Cain by her mate, Samael (Shaitan) the Dragon. Lilith appeared in Sumerian times as a Goddess of the Beasts of the Wild, as well as Sorcery and Night-fornication. Lilith was said to have many forms, from beautiful women to half human and the bottom half animal, to half woman and half flame. Lilith is also the mother of demons and a Vampyric spirit which is a primal manifestation of the Zoroastrian and Manichaean AZ and Jeh. Lilith may also be related to the Indian KALI, whose name is one of Her 17 names.

Luciferian – A Luciferian is an individual who recognizes the associative spiritual traits of the God/ess within. Luciferians do not worship Satan but recognize there must be balance between the material and spiritual, the darkness and light. Luciferians view their own being as holding the Black Flame of Lucifer – Samael and Lilith within, this is intellect and wisdom. This is beyond good and evil, the spirit has two aspects – the demonic (instinct, desire) and angelic (intelligence, consciousness).

Luciferian Magick – Essentially close to the term, Black Magick but specifically focuses on ascending in a self-deified and isolated way in reference to Lucifer, the bringer of Light. Luciferian Magick may in this term make reference to seeking Light and darkness through magickal development, not an abstract concept, but to manifest the Will in both the spiritual and physical world.

Magick - To Ascend and Become. In a Luciferian sense, Magick is to strengthen, develop and initiate the self through balanced forms of Willed Change.

OVLM HQLIPVTh - Olahm Ha-Qliphoth [Hebrew] – the world of matter in which we live in, created by the desire of the Adversary being Samael and Lilith. The elements of this book if found and utilized in the context of its writing, displays possibilities via initiation to encircle, control and manifest the desire of the Luciferian.

Paitisha/Paityara [Avestan/Pahlavi] – A daeva/druj which is counteraction, antinomianism and opposition. This spirit is a manifestation of the Luciferian current of both Ahriman and Az, complimented/strengthed by Aeshma or the result of the path, Heshem.

Predatory Spiritualism – The act of devouring spiritual energy and making the Adept stronger from ritual practice, the act of encircling spiritual energy either symbolically or literally based on theistic or non-theistic belief, once encircling the spirit or deific mask, symbolically devouring and consuming the association of the spirit into the self. May be attributed to the inner practices of the Black Order of the Dragon. A ritual published in Luciferian Witchcraft, The Ritual of Druj Nasu is a vampiric or predatory rite utilizing ancient Persian sorcery inversions and techniques of sorcery for strengthening consciousness.

Qlippoth - As the Zohar attributes the Qlippoth as being a result of the Separation from creation it seems by mere definition that the Qlippoth is indeed inherent of the concept of the Black Flame, or Gift of Samael. Between two separate things, there is a concept of Separation which essentially is the concept of 'shells' or 'peels' being the aspects the sorcerer must fill and in turn devour in the process of becoming like Samael and Lilith. The Qlippoth and Tree of Death (Da'ath) is the pathway to becoming like the Adversary, as the Tree of Life is the path to joining with God (becoming one with).

Sabbat – The gathering and conclave of sorcerers. There are in a conceptual sense, two types of Sabbats – the Luciferian and the Infernal. The Infernal is a bestial and earth-bound journey, similar to those shown in woodcuts and gathering points. The Infernal Sabbat is sometimes sexual, where the sorcerer may shape shift and communicate with their familiars and spirits. The Luciferian Sabbat is a solar and air phenomena based in dreaming, floating in air and having sensations of a warm heat similar to sitting out in the sun. The Luciferian Sabbat is a strengthening and development of the Body of Light, the astral double of the Adept.

Sabbatic – A term which is related as the knowledge of the secret gathering, the Sabbat. This is a focus of inspired teaching based on magickal development via dreaming and astral projection. The Sabbat is the gathering of sorcerers in dreaming flesh, when the body is shed for the psyche which is able to go forth in whatever form it desires. The witch or sorcerer who is able to attend the Sabbat has already freed the mind through a process of Antinomian magical practice, thus enforcing and strengthening the imagination as a visualization tool, similar to divination and 'sight' with spirits.

Shades – Spirits of the Dead, ghosts and phantoms which walks in the astral plane. These spirits may represent in some cases the body of the sorcerer in the plane of the dead, a world separate in some areas from our own living perception. In evocation and necromantical practice, the shades are brought around and closer to the world of the living.

Sorcery – The art of encircling energy and power of self, by means of self -fascination (inspiration through the imagination). Sorcery is a willed controlling of energies of a magical current, which is responsive through the Will and Belief of the sorcerer. While sorcery is the encircling or ensorcerling of power around the self, Magick is the Willed change of ones objective universe.

Staota [Avestan/Pahlavi] – A Vibration which could cause death or some change, that which would encircle the one sounding the Staota in self-focused energy. A Staota is used historically in the mythological tale, The Matigan-I Yosht-I Fryan. A Sorcerous technique presented in the Second Edition of YATUK DINOIH.

Tiamat [Assyrian] – Generative concept from which all emerged from. Tiamat is a feminine dragon principle whose brood were half insect, beast or serpent. Tiamat is viewed as the vampire goddess in the Luciferian Path.

Therion [Greek] – The Beast Refers to the hidden aspects of the mind.

Tishin [Avestan/Pahlavi] – A demon of thirst or vampyric/luciferian druj, serpent and daemon. Tishin is related to the concept of desire for continued existence, thus immortality and separation of the self from the objective world. This concept is within the gnosis of Predatory Spirituality and relates the Luciferian to seek to expand the mind by initiation, to manifest his/her desire on earth.

Vampirism/Vampyrism – The act of consuming Chi or Anghuya in a ritualized setting. Life or energy force is found in all things, the sorcerer practicing vampirism would encircle and consume to grow stronger with this energy. Practitioners of Vampirism DO create their own Chi but also use Chi absorbed or drained from other sources to manipulate the shadow by dream and ritual, growing stronger. The Eye is both a symbol of vampirism and Luciferian practice, predatory spirituality. Vampirism is based in the foundations of early Egyptian texts and Charles Darwin theories of natural selection. Not referring to the Religion of Vampirism. See PREDATORY SPIRITUALISM.

Yatukih [Avestan/Pahlavi] – Term denoting relevance of sorcery within Persian mythology. Directly relating to the title of the practice of Ahrimanic/Satanic sorcery and the practitioner in a modern sense. See "Yatuk Dinoih".

Yatuk Dinoih [Avestan/Pahlavi] – Witchcraft and Sorcery. The development and practice of adversarial and opposing sorcery to encircle the witch or wizard in self-developed energy. The principle of Darkness and the Deva/Druj (Demon) worship of this sect was in seeming model form, that by becoming as Darkness they developed a Light within. See LUCIFERIAN WITCHCRAFT - Grimoire written by Michael Ford.

Yatus [Avestan/Pahlavi] – A group of 'demons' or sorcerers who practice Yatukih sorcery and Daeva-Yasna. The Yatus were led by Akht-Jadu, Akhtya. They were also considered nomads in nature, wandering through all parts of Persia practicing their religion. This term has no considerations to the Zoroastrian religion, while the modern and separate practices described in Liber HVHI and parts of Luciferian Witchcraft are manifestations of a new type of interpretation of the practice of Daeva-Yasna.

Yezidi [Kurdish]– Considered 'devil worshippers' by outsiders, the Yezidi are those who are dedicated to Malak Tauus, the Peacock Angel, also called Shaitan or Lucifer. In the MESHAF RESH, the Black Book, Azazel is the first angel, created before any other. He is considered most beautiful and is the one who teaches and enlightens humanity. In the areas of Yatuk Dinoih, Sabbatic and Luciferian Sorcery, transformation occurs by the embrace and becoming of the opposing force, or adversarial (antinomian) ideas within the self. The initiate moves through the magical current to strengthen his or her own being. In a modern context, Malak (Angel) Tauus (Peacock) is the symbol of solar enlightenment, wisdom and beautiful developed being.

DEDICATION

I wish to thank Priest Dualkarnain for his support, editing assistance and development within THE ORDER OF PHOSPHORUS. Hope Marie who is an excellent partner. All Council of Arezura brothers and sisters who have worked so had to guide the growth of the Order in 2007.

ABOUT THE AUTHOR

Michael W. Ford is the author of numerous books and publications on the Left Hand Path and Magick. Michael is the founder of THE ORDER OF PHOSPHORUS and THE BLACK ORDER OF THE DRAGON.

Made in the USA
San Bernardino, CA
11 October 2014